THE MAKING OF
AN ENGLISH COUNTRY GARDEN

The Making of
An English Country Garden

———

DEBORAH KELLAWAY

Photographs by
JERRY HARPUR

Garden plans by
HESTER ROBINSON

Chatto & Windus
LONDON

Published in 1990
by Chatto & Windus Ltd
20 Vauxhall Bridge Road
London SW1V 2SA

A CIP catalogue record for this book
is available from the British Library.

ISBN 0-7011-3535-2

First published in hardback in 1988
by Chatto & Windus

Text copyright © Deborah Kellaway 1988
Photographs copyright © Jerry Harpur 1988

Deborah Kellaway has asserted her right to be
identified as the author of this work

Photoset in Linotron Sabon by
Rowland Phototypesetting Ltd
Bury St Edmunds, Suffolk
Text printed in Great Britain by
Mackays of Chatham PLC, Chatham, Kent
Plates printed by White Quill Press
Mitcham, Surrey

Contents

To Bill
il miglior fabbro

List of illustrations and plates

The photographs were taken
in August 1987

Acknowledgements

'I hope you're not copying it out of another book,' said my youngest child sternly when I sat working on the first draft of my manuscript, one finger in the pages of an open gardening book, other books and catalogues all round me on the floor.

And of course, the garden itself *is* copied out of books, and would have been a poor thing without them. I hasten now to name, with gratitude, the writers who have influenced me most, shaping my taste, teaching me about plants, instructing me in horticultural skills and giving me contented hours of armchair gardening.

First comes Russell Page. *The Education of a Gardener* (Collins, 1962) was *my* gardening education and I have tried to describe what this has meant in chapter III of this book.

Next comes V. Sackville-West, from whom I learnt to make the edges of my borders straight and the planting within them exuberant. I know bits of *Even More for Your Garden* (Michael Joseph, 1958) by heart.

It was Vita Sackville-West's warm review of *We Made a Garden* by Margery Fish (L. Collingridge, 1956) which introduced me to the writings of that now famous plantswoman. I made faithful notes from her *Cottage Garden Flowers* (L. Collingridge, 1961) when I began to plant this garden.

Robin Lane Fox's stylish books, *Better Gardening*, (R. & L., 1982) and *Variations on a Garden* (R. & L., 1986) are a pleasure to read, and the discovery that many of his 'better' plants are my chosen plants has been gratifying. His favourite hardy annuals are becoming mine.

To have Alan Bloom's six-acre show garden at Bressingham almost within walking distance of this cottage was a very great stroke of luck, and his mixtures of clearly-labelled perennial flowers in island beds stretching between lawns almost as far as the eye could see was an instant education, providing one came armed with pencil and notebook on a summer Sunday afternoon. To reinforce the visual learning, I bought Alan Bloom's *Perennials for Trouble-free Gardening* (Faber, 1960), which remains to this day my most authoritative guide to herbaceous perennials.

As a simple yet comprehensive handbook to answer a whole range of questions, I used and still use *The Small Garden* by Brigadier E. Lucas Philips (Pan Books, new edition, 1969). Its mixture of information with informality is also to be found in the books of Christopher Lloyd. His is a humorous and friendly voice, masking formidable horticultural experience. His throwaway recommendations become my command, and I follow advice given in *The Well-Tempered Garden* (Penguin Books, 1978), *The Adventurous Gardener* (Allen Lane, 1983) and the beautifully illustrated *The Year at Great Dixter* (Viking, 1987).

I have read and re-read *The Englishwoman's Garden*, edited by Alvilde Lees-Milne and Rosemary Verey (Chatto & Windus, 1980) because its thirty-six women gardeners describe their gardening tribulations and aspirations so convincingly. So do the same editors' thirty-three male authors in *The Englishman's Garden* (Allen Lane, 1982). Most of the gardens in these two books are rather grand, but the cottage gardener can poach ideas from them.

For help in special areas of the garden, I have leant on specialist books. J. Fisk's *Success with Clematis* (The Garden Book Club, 1962) is mentioned gratefully in Chapter iv of this book. Frances Perry's classic *Water Gardens* (Penguin, 1985) was my guide to the planting of the pond, and Brian Furner's *The Kitchen Garden* (Pan Books, 1966) remains our guide to vegetable gardening. Peter Beales' grand *Classic Roses* (Collins Harvill, 1985) is now my treasured encyclopaedia of old roses.

East Anglia is rich in nurserymen, some of whom produce catalogues which rank with my most-thumbed garden books. In particular, *Notcutt's Book of Plants* in its enlarged edition of 1983 is indispensable to me.

I list here the first-rate nurseries, now also garden centres, that have supplied our garden with its plants ever since Notcutt's delivered our first thirty-five trees.

Trees and shrubs
Notcutt's Nurseries Ltd, Woodbridge, Suffolk
Notcutt's Garden Centre, Daniels Road, Norwich, Norfolk

Roses
Peter Beales' Roses, London Road, Attleborough, Norfolk
E. B. Le Grice (Roses) Ltd, Norwich Road, North Walsham, Norfolk

Herbaceous perennials
Bressingham Gardens, Diss, Norfolk
Beth Chatto, White Barn House, Elmstead Market, Colchester, Essex
Moores' Nurseries, Bressingham, Diss, Norfolk

Clematis
Fisk's Clematis Nursery, Westleton, Nr Saxmundham, Suffolk

Aquatics
Waveney Fish Farm, Victoria Road, Diss, Norfolk

Seeds
S. E. Marshall & Co. Ltd, Regal Road, Wisbech, Cambs
Thompson & Morgan, London Road, Ipswich, Suffolk

Finally, I must thank my friend Marilyn McBriar whose advice is now translated into a fastigiate beech and a tiered yew hedge.

I

The Site

___

The 'Particulars' said: 'The grounds extend to half an acre. There is a carefully planned herbaceous border. The rest is mostly put down to lawns.' It sounded invitingly mature and cared-for. But I only went to see the place for purposes of comparison, to prove some point about its modest price. My first visit belonged in the strictly fantasy class, where one *pretends* one might buy a weekend cottage in the country.

The cottage was pretty, built sideways onto a narrow lane, thatched, newly painted white inside and out. Its owner had bought it, condemned and derelict, three years before, had done it up, and then decided not to live in it. It had originally been two semi-detached cottages, and was L-shaped at the back. You went through a little black iron gate and round the end of the cottage to find a door in the angle of the 'L'. Inside was a sitting room with old, unvarnished beams. I stood looking out of a window with the owner. The land stretched away over flattish ground until it stopped, abruptly, at an overgrown, scrubby hedge. It was a view of what looked like waste land – knee-high grass and weeds, unbroken by shrub or tree, but only by a bumpy gravel path which led straight to an old, tiled shed, where once a donkey had been kept.

'Where is the herbaceous border?'

'Ah,' he replied with pride and amusement, pointing his finger. 'Do you see some yellow over there? That's it! It's all there. We had it laid out for us by the famous nursery gardens up the road. You've only got to cut the grass and you'll find it.'

'You've only got to cut the grass,' his wife repeated. 'Get an Allen scythe – two cuts and it'll be a lawn.'

We went outside, down the bumpy path to the old donkey shed. Looking back towards its western front, we could see that

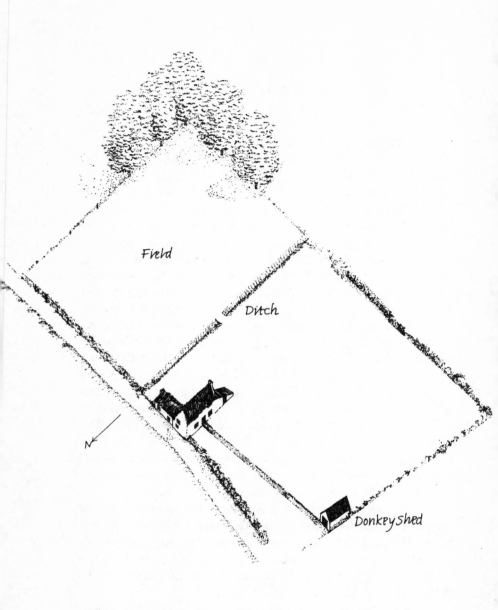

Field

Ditch

N

Donkey Shed

The site as we found it.

the cottage had an endearing, squat little face, two upstairs windows like eyes under curved thatched eyebrows. But the surroundings were bleak: half an acre of nothing, nothing to filter the East Anglian wind blowing strongly across it. And beyond the half acre, to north, east and west, lay various manifestations of the outside world.

To the north there was an 'A' road; it ran along the far side of a large field opposite the cottage, its succession of travelling lorries silhouetted against the sky. Also silhouetted against the skyline was a high, new, red brick house with a formidable tiled roof.

To the east lay a building plot, separated from the cottage by a ditch. The estate agents claimed that building permission had been granted and it was to be sold separately. If a house went up there, you would almost be able to hear its occupants cleaning their teeth in the mornings. At present, it was a neglected field of a third of an acre belonging to the cottage, and round its furthest corner five tall, silvery willows grew. Beyond it, set well back from the lane, was a long white cottage that had once been a poultry farm. Derelict hen sheds and fowl runs peeped between elder bushes.

To the west there was another white-washed cottage – a small dairy farm, surrounded by a variety of cow sheds with rusty iron roofs.

To the south there was only the overgrown hedge; its hawthorns, elders, willows and hazels had grown into bushy trees, tied together with brambles, preventing further view.

I went back to London and told my family about the lovely big-beamed sitting room within and the desert without. I knew that there is a lot you can do to an indifferent house, but there is no way of making a view where there isn't one. If you are buying a country cottage, the cottage is less important than the country round it; this one had its priorities wrong. Still, my husband and eight-year-old daughter went up to see it. My daughter picked up a very special flint on the old path. My husband, returning, said: 'No,' then added, doubtfully: 'If you really want to make a garden somewhere, you could do it there.'

'But how?' I asked, astonished and secretly pleased. 'I don't see how you could divide it up? It doesn't *lend* itself to anything. It hasn't even got a front garden and a back garden. It doesn't *suggest* anything. Or rather, all it suggests to me,' I added, talking myself into it, 'is that the bit inside the L-shape should be paved with brick, to look like an old courtyard.'

We made a very low offer, as a way of leaving the whole affair in fantasy territory, and were soon informed, to our relief, that someone else had bought the place.

One morning, two months later, as we were setting off to Suffolk to stay in the borrowed cottage of some friends (a much more trouble-free arrangement), we had a letter from the estate agent informing us that the vendor had now accepted our offer, as his other purchaser had backed out. In consternation we drove from the borrowed cottage to the empty one to establish one thing only: was there, could there be, beyond the overgrown southern boundary hedge, a view?

It was now high June, and high indeed were the weeds, shoulder high now, vicious and painful, stinging, scratching, pricking and clinging, as we thrashed our way through them down the half acre to the boundary. Bravely we reached the line of hedge, at least twelve feet high, with a shorter hedge of nettles at its feet. We stamped on the nettles, reached forward, broke twigs, held back branches, scratched our arms on thorns, finally managed to peep through. On the other side there was a meadow, then another overgrown hedge – no houses to be seen; it was peaceful pasture. On our way back up the gentle slope, pushing through the ferocious weeds, we once more looked for the herbaceous border; the yellow had disappeared, but there was a flash of blue.

So we wrote back to the estate agent and said that our offer still held if the vendor would include in the sale the neighbouring field with its building permission as well. We thought this proviso might prove our escape route. But by now he was as anxious to sell as we were reluctant to buy. Wearily he agreed that the building plot should be ours at no extra cost. It was thus that cottage, grounds and neighbouring field became ours for £3,600 in the summer of 1965. We did not know, when we signed the contract, that we had bought an acre of light, fertile, neutral soil, tilted slightly towards the sun.

II

The Grass and the Weeds

We arrived at the beginning of the summer holidays with three children, a dog, my husband's brother and his wife and useful van. Inside the van was a Hayterette, a small rotary mower. We sat outside the cottage and knew what we had to do. We had to build up the north side of our land, plant trees quickly and thickly along the side where the 'A' road and the brick house stood against the sky. We had to plant until we could not see that skyline any more. Then we had to open up the south – not too much at first, or the bleakness on all sides would be intolerable. But as the view to the north was blotted out, so we could allow ourselves a little more to the south until finally the northern aspect would be obliterated and the south wide open. In short, we had to reverse the view.

We started, that first day, by axing an elder bush on the southern boundary ditch. A glimpse of water meadow appeared under the branches of a willow tree. We got the brand new rotary mower out of the van and for the rest of the afternoon the men took it in turns to cut a long, diagonal swathe through the weeds from the house to the little patch of view. The weeds were much higher than the children: spreading, soft, shimmery colonies of nettles, with white or mauve flowers; thistles of all sorts: milky thistles, creeping thistles, three feet high in colonies, but towering above all these, wicked, branching five foot thistles with stems like trunks, tough, dry, prickly and hollow, crude little purple thistle flowers on top. We did not know the names of the other weeds, and they were all the more menacing and alien because of this. But the whole effect was far from the bright green of grass; it was muted, the dullest of grey-greens in August, nettle-green, tinged with brown, the typical harvest of neglected land. Among the really towering plants, taller even than the tallest thistles, must have been hemlock, poisonous and smelling, so the wild-flower books tell me now, of mice. But the smell of those mingled weeds as the Hayterette began its massacre was intoxicatingly pungent and sweet, the crushed and mangled stems giving off an intense, juicy vegetable scent.

The Hayterette was advertised as cutting long grass as well as short. During the next weeks and months it cut down our wilderness of weeds and it is still alive in our shed, awaiting the day when a more sophisticated machine balks at some tricky bank or corner to be cleared. Of course it was not the right tool for the job; of course we should have bought, or hired, a motor scythe or found a true countryman to cut the whole area for us by swinging his old-fashioned scythe round in the way that looks so relaxed and rhythmic and that is in fact so tiring and difficult to the unskilled. It took my husband the whole summer holiday – four weeks – to cut the weeds in the garden; the field had to wait until the next year. He used the Hayterette as a battering ram, pushing it forwards against the strongest growths; slowly they would topple, slant and crash; back he would pull the rotary mower and then forward again, travelling over the fallen corpses and chopping them with that stout revolving blade into little mangled bits. Sometimes there was seedling elder and willow to be overcome. It took about an hour to do a few square yards; the Hayterette is not self-propelled, it is man-propelled. Every now and then, the chopped-up wreckage had to be raked up into huge piles, wheeled away and burnt. However, by the end of the holiday we could walk anywhere in the garden without a struggle and look about us. '*That's* better,' we said.

But it was not better. It was worse. The weeds, waving sombre in the breeze, looked better than this flat tousled stubble of tussocks. It was not a garden; it was an enormous, very slightly tilted rectangle of dead-coloured ground with nothing to break the monotony or momentarily arrest the eye as it travelled across the space and came to rest on the cottage itself, looking uncomfortably high and dominant with its steep thatched gable and bare white walls rising strongly out of the horizontal plane. I felt defensive when visiting friends came and, having stumbled over the rough ground to the southern boundary, we would turn to face that unavoidable northward view, the road, the wind-swept space, and a complicated electric pylon providing a vertical landmark to the right. To cover the bleak moment, I would launch into a hasty account of how we intended to 'plant out' the northward view, of how we would plant trees, of how we would gradually remove the southern hedge, of how at present the setting was wrong but we would re-orientate it and make it right. The whole thing sounded too long-term to be convincing.

Next spring, we drove down from London and drew up beside the cottage one evening to find the whole place trans-formed: all the ditches and hedges were frilled with white lace; the cow parsley was out. It heralded a change in our weeds; now that the stinging and prickling monsters were controlled (and that spring we watered the nettles along the ditches with brush-wood killer) gentler weeds took their place; by midsummer the tall, elegant meadowsweet, wild relation of spiraea, was grow-ing with Norfolk reeds in the bottoms of the ditches; I had never met it before, and wondered at first what the lovely scent was. There were poppies, chamomile, scarlet pimpernel, purple self-heal, blue speedwell, sheets of buttercups, daisies and ground ivy flowering in the grass. Above all, there was grass now; grass was the most pervasive and welcome of the weeds. We did not sow grass seed, except in two small, re-shaped areas later on; we simply cut the tall weeds as we had been advised to do, and went on cutting them, and gradually the grass came. Perhaps it had been there all the time; certainly, of all weeds, it is the one that positively thrives on cutting. It was still depressingly rough and tussocky in our second summer, but in our third, wide spaces began to look green and smooth.

Originally I dreamt of leaving most of it long and cutting it, as

meadow-gardeners advise, three or four times a year; I envis-
aged a paradise garden, like the garden in the foreground of a
medieval painting, where all manner of flowers seem to be
embroidered amongst the grass; I planned to supplement the
wild flowers by sowing and naturalising choice bulbs and
biennials; I made a beginning by scattering seeds of honesty in
likely places. But memories of his recent struggle with the long
growth made my husband oppose this idea. Having got the stuff
short, he wanted to keep it short. He would rather drive a
hundred miles from London every fortnight in the growing
season to cut the grass than let it grow really long again.

So that was what happened. For the next four years he went
on cutting the whole half-acre nearly every fortnight with the
Hayterette. The grass cuttings lay in swathes along the surface.
Occasionally, when they were particularly thick, we raked them
up. The cutting job used to take at least three hours, and a lot of
energy. After four years, we bought a 5 hp Hayter, wider than
the Hayterette and self-propelled. It proceeded along the ground
at its own dignified pace and the job still took a long time to
complete, but was less tiring. Five more years passed, and my
son was competent to wield a rotary mower. At first he enjoyed
this promotion, then showed signs of wearying. We bribed him
to continue by investing in a 7 hp ride-on Mountfield with a
twenty four inch cut. He worked out the most economical route
round the grass, the one that entailed least reversing. This
evolved as a sweeping, circular progression, spiralling inwards
in concentric rings until it ended in a triumphantly executed
figure-of-eight. The grass could now be cut in only one hour – or
an hour and a half, on the days when the field had to be done too.

And it continued to improve. But the more it improved, the
more it tyrannised. I began to feel discontented with it, fussy
about it, to hanker after a weekly cut. I learnt to pull the
Mountfield's stubborn starting cord myself so that I could do
the job when no-one else was there. I bought a pair of long-
handled edging shears at a local auction sale. These proved a

total success, sounding like superbly expensive dress-maker's scissors when they cut a sharp edge to the grass. They seemed able to slice through tight-packed soil as well as turf. They made the place look comparatively tended, almost groomed. Then I bought a sweeper, revolving nylon brushes and a huge yellow canvas grass-box which had to be pushed over the bumpy ground while the dusty cuttings flew up into my eyes. Then suddenly a long piece of grass would wind itself into the ball-bearings and the whole thing would come to a halt; a very tiring tool, though a necessary one if there was to be a real lawn.

But there was not a real lawn. Just as the vision of some sort of greensward became almost a reality, the moles arrived; the little pyramids of dark brown earth multiplied until there were molehills everywhere. We tried sticking mothballs down the runs – a useless manoeuvre; we tried expensive smoke 'bombs', but it appears that these are only effective if you can dig down far enough, and cunningly enough, to smoke out the moles' main run; to smoke the tributary passages will not kill the moles. Then we tried mole traps; it was months before we had any success with them, and to this day our success is only partial; even when you are sure you are placing them in a freshly worked run, pointing in the right direction and lightly balanced so that they are free to snap shut, you will probably not catch your mole. (And of course, if you do, you will feel a brutal bully.) One morning we watched a neighbouring farmer's wife at work; she stood with a spade in a meadow, watching for the ground to move; she knew the exact hours, morning and evening, when the moles are at work. At the critical moment she pounced, with deadly aim, spading them out. Soon the barbed wire fences were strung with moleskins.

I could not do this. Instead, I have reached a sort of truce with moles. After all, their network of tunnels drains and aereates the lawn; the soil they dig out is beautifully sifted. The only thing wrong with it is that it is on the grass. Remove it, then, I have told myself, shovel it up wherever you find it, before it has killed the grass beneath, put it in a barrow and trundle it across the garden to a flower bed. Tip it out and spread it with a rake. The resulting top-dressing will hide weeds, will look like minutely expert cultivation, and will give the old border soil a refreshing instant boost.

Our latest tool is a strimmer, a powered wonder whose rapidly revolving nylon thread clean-shaves long grasses along ditches, under hedges, round trees with one swipe of its rotating head. Once you own a strimmer, your standards of neatness rise alarmingly, and when it breaks down from overwork you find you cannot live without it, and have to buy another.

So now the grass is reasonably flat, but pock-marked with bald patches where the molehills were. Should we now do more to it? Should we treat it with hormone weedkiller in spring, then over-seed it in August with fine grass seed, which might gradually take the place of the buttercup, couch and clover? Should we be more enterprising with its contours, moulding it with a hired bulldozer into a gentle valley which would lead the eye towards the view? Should we at least spike it, roll it?

So far we have done none of these things. We tell ourselves that our meadow grass survives drought better than fine lawn mixtures do; then we tell ourselves that *next* year, if the spring is wet, it will look better. When I discover a cowslip in the grass I gratefully transplant it to a safer place. Half an hour's hunt will usually yield a four-leaf clover for those in need of luck. The thing is a compromise; we do try to cut it once a week now, in the growing season, but bouncing round on the Mountfield for an hour is not exhausting, and the smell of cut grass is sweet.

It still cannot be called a lawn, but from a certain distance, after cutting, in the afternoon light, it looks like one.

III

The Trees

___

All the clearing and cutting, poisoning, chopping and burning, is the destructive side of gardening, the aggressive 'I'm master here, you brutes' attitude. It carries sharp satisfaction along with its exhaustion. Most people, moving into a new garden, indulge in it, even if (or particularly if) they have never gardened in their lives before. There is a strong urge to dig out whatever is there, and I have sadly watched neighbours moving into old gardens and grubbing up plants which, years before, I had watched their predecessors lovingly plant. There are, indeed, two sorts of gardener; the clean sweepers and the conservers. But one thing is certain; you will never make a nice garden by simply digging things up; you can only make a nice garden by planting things. And if time is short on a spring morning and there is a choice to be made between weeding a flower bed or sowing a row of seeds, I would fix my thoughts on how the garden will look in six weeks' time and choose to sow the seeds.

There was nothing whatever to conserve in our Norfolk garden, except for the five huge cricket bat willows (*Salix* × *Caerulea*) in the corner of the field, and the invisible herbaceous border if ever I could find it. So there was everything to plant. And, if our dream of the 'reversed view' was to be realised, we had to start with trees.

It was fortunate that I had read Russell Page's classic, *The Education of a Gardener*, before the planting began. Otherwise, like most amateurs, I would have indulged exclusively in 'dot' planting, one of this and one of that – never more than one of each. A sort of greed to have a specimen of everything that I loved, or that was loved by somebody whose gardening book I admired, would have governed all my choices. But I learnt, from Russell Page, that five trees of the same species will often look better than one tree from each of five different species. Nature knows this: her effects are simple, repetitive and massed. One plant of cow parsley is nothing; it was the massed effect of hundreds of plants of cow parsley along the hedgerows and ditches that first took my breath away. Similarly the reason why an orchard looks so nice, or an avenue of limes or beeches, is that the trees used to make the effect are all the same.

When I explained this principle to my daughter recently she replied: 'But I thought our garden *was* "One-of-Everything".' I was annoyed, but have to confess that my Education as a Gardener has been incomplete and, over the years, greed has got the better of me and many single specimens have crept in. At least we did try hard, in our original plantings, to achieve simplicity.

One must, as Russell Page explains so persuasively, decide upon a governing idea, a theme, which will best suit the character of one's plot, and choose one's plants to express that theme. It was not difficult to decide what idea should govern our plantings: it should be the idea of the English cottage garden. We had to wed the picturesque domesticity of our cottage to the large quiet spaces of the landscape; the trees we planted near it must not be too tall, and must look as if they had always grown there – or as if their forebears might have grown there two hundred years ago, when the lath and plaster cottage was still young. The answer seemed obvious: we would plant fruit trees. And the word 'English' was important, too; exotic trees recently imported from distant lands must be resisted, or at least played down; we must choose not beautiful Japanese flowering cherries, but beautiful native cherries instead. And so, at first, we did. But here I made a rudimentary mistake: I chose my native cherries, not at first hand, but out of a nurseryman's catalogue. *Prunus avium* 'Plena', the double white form of our native wild cherry, was described in my much-thumbed handbook as 'a floral glory'. I had never seen it, but ordered three, and we planted them along the ditch that separates the garden from the

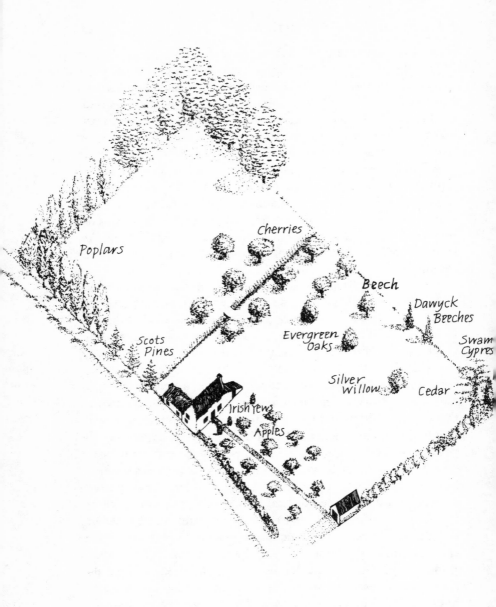

Our first planting of trees.

field. It is not that I don't like them now – I suppose they are a kind of 'glory', large and domed or pyramidal in shape with dangling clusters of large white double flowers in May. It is just that I have subsequently seen, and indeed bought, cherries that suit our cottage garden better. They come in a different section of the catalogue – not under 'Trees', but under 'Fruit'. For they are eating cherries; not only is there the hope that one day we shall beat the birds to them and have a harvest of dessert cherries, black and red, to eat, but their blossom is beautiful in an effortless and unpretentious way; it does not dangle so much as cluster; and the trees' shape is looser, less stiffly formal, than *P. avium* 'Plena'. For purposes of pollination we had to plant two different varieties, 'Early Rivers' and 'Governor Wood', and it is the blossom of 'Governor Wood' that is particularly lovely, like clotted cream along the branches. Writers of books on fruit growing always dissuade the amateur gardener from fruiting cherries, saying that they grow too big to be suitable for the average garden. But their size seemed to us, with our large empty space to fill, a positive advantage. We planted them near the three *aviums*, further down the field. My main quarrel with these five cherries now is that black fly attack their growing tips, and in a bad year one can see the curled up scorched brown shoots from far away.

But I have another quarrel with them: they blossom too late for the Easter holidays, when we can enjoy our spring garden most. I had planned to have white cherry blossom to form a complementary canopy over daffodils in the April grass. I decided we must have more cherries, earlier cherries, a second row, parallel to the first, but growing down the nearside of the ditch and thus in line with our kitchen window, so that we could gaze at them as we ate our breakfast at the kitchen table in April or in March. One spring day I saw a dreamlike cherry tree blooming in the court of Clare College, Cambridge, when the daffodils were at their best all along the Backs. It was *Prunus* × *yedoensis*, dense with flowers, white and weeping. Japanese or no, I ordered it. Then I ordered the famous *Prunus sargentii*, because it is earlier still, March flowering; its cool pink single flower buds burst with the earliest daffodils, and its flaming red leaves in September are the most reliably brilliant autumn colour that I know. And then I bought *Prunus subhirtella* 'Autumnalis', whose delicately fragile single white flowers come not only in early spring, but throughout the winter too. So there it was; what started, in the autumn of 1965, as a simple planting of three white cherries along a ditch, became, six years later, a double row of eight cherries, seven white and one pink, and I could not even say to myself: 'Never mind – they *are* all cherries,' because at the end of the second row I had slipped in a medlar, having fallen in love with its gnarled shape and leathery leaves on a nursery field.

Fruit trees remained our theme. We longed to produce crops – apples, above all. We decided, from the start, to plant out the offending skyline on one side of the cottage with apple trees, and we began with three, two bush and one standard, in the autumn of 1965. We planted them parallel with the gravel path that led down to our shed.

The next year, we decided that three apple trees were not enough; when we looked up from the bottom of the garden towards the skyline, the young trees made no difference at all. We planted three more on the other side of the path; the pattern was the same, two bush, one standard in the middle. We lined them up with the first ones as carefully as we could. Four years later, we saw that our planting was still too timid, too miserly – the lorries could still be heard and seen, and we planted three more apples, all standards, parallel to our first two rows but on the other side of the front lawn; we added two standard plums and a crab apple 'John Downie'. So we had a little orchard: eleven fruit trees planted as symmetrically as the site allowed between the front face of the cottage and the shed.

Despite a series of dry springs, they grew quite well; but then, one spring, we panicked. A new bungalow appeared on a neighbouring field to the north of the lane and we rushed to reinforce our orchard, planting with semi-mature fastigiate trees squeezed in near to the hedge. I chose them growing on their nursery field; Notcutt's of Woodbridge issued a duplicated list of semi-mature trees on offer and, with price in mind, I chose three hawthorns (there was a lot of hawthorn in the hedge already) *Crataegus monogyna* 'Stricta'; they are slim and upright like lombardy poplars, but not nearly as tall, and they have pretty white blossom amongst their typical hawthorn leaves. We added two standard hawthorns, *Crataegus* × *prunifolia*, planted close to the cottage on either side where gaps in the hedge made us particularly vulnerable. These trees looked temptingly mature and suitably indigenous and unshowy, though we had never heard of them before; their leaves, as the name implies, are rather like a pear's, shiny and rather dark; there are panicles of white flowers in June and orange berries, like rose hips, hang deep into the winter. They go well with the mixed hedge, well with the apple trees. But I doubt if the rush to buy semi-mature trees was sensible. One of the fastigiate hawthorns almost died, and had to grow all over again from its rootstock, which turned out not to be fastigiate; the others seemed shocked into years of comparative inactivity by their sudden transplantation. They are barely as tall as the bush apples now and will ultimately make the apples feel hemmed in. But at least we have now achieved our primary aim; we have obliterated the view to the north. After ten years, not a vestige of the old harsh skyline could be seen, and the bungalow roof disappeared.

It was ten years, too, before our apple trees fruited properly. Before that, sometimes one young tree would bear quite promisingly, sometimes another, but we began to despair of bumper crops. Then, just as we were beginning to say, 'Apples are too difficult for amateurs,' the miracle happened, and after twelve or thirteen years all the trees are laden, their branches curtseying to the ground in August and September with the weight of fruit.

We pour cornucopias of apples into stout paper sacks and store them anxiously in cold rooms.

We chose our trees to supply fruit from August to March. The first to ripen is 'Scarlet Pimpernel', a shapely standard tree, whose apples are sweeter than those of 'Beauty of Bath', the familiar old 'early' which is now superseded. 'Scarlet Pimpernel' has, in fact, a deeply blushing crimson cheek on an almost cream-coloured skin. 'George Cave' comes next, a better apple, sweeter, tastier; towards the end of August it bears a lovely, lavish crop of pale green apples painted all over with brush strokes of rosy red. Neither of these early, summer-holiday apples is disease-prone; instead, alas, they are pest-prone, for their season coincides with that of the wasps. One is supposed to be able to find wasps' nests by carefully observing the direction in which they fly, but so far we have not achieved this. I used to trap dozens in jam jars with a spoonful of sticky jam in the bottom of each, making a squalid ring round the base of the tree, but now, at last, our crop is so big that we can afford to share it with the wasps and still find all the apples we want to eat. How lovely it is, in August, to be able to say goodbye to the softening 'Golden Delicious' apples from the shops. An apple eaten straight from the tree has a crisp juiciness that cannot be stored, and when you rub your thumb over its skin, it squeaks.

1 a) **A view of the cottage:** standing in the ditch behind a clump of meadowsweet you look up the grassy slope which, when the shadows lengthen, is almost a lawn. You cannot see the 'A' road on the skyline any more behind the 20-year-old trees.

1 b) **The view from the cottage:** you sit outside the cottage and look down the slope towards the water meadows. This is the view round which we gradually arranged our sight-lines, cutting a swathe of grass through the extended herbaceous border to invite a walk towards the view. The hedgerow oak is framed by two Dawyck beeches on the left and one on the right (here hidden by the willow, the sort of thing that happens when you plant a lot of trees.) In the foreground an Irish yew marks the corner of the cottage.

After 'George Cave' comes 'Worcester', familiar, ripening in
September, prolific, dark red, bearing its fruits towards the tips
of its branches and therefore demanding light pruning. It has
beautiful blossom but a tendency to scab. And so, unhappily,
have our next two apples, 'Ellison's Orange' and 'Cox's Orange
Pippin', ripening in mid-September and November respectively;
Cox is world famous; Ellison's is our favourite, indescribably
juicy when eaten off the tree – you can almost drink the juice as
you bite. But I wish I had known about the difficulty of dealing
with scab when we planted our apples; it is slightly heart-
sinking to offer people apples with black spots and blotches on
their cheeks. There *are* scab-resistant varieties; it would be
sensible for amateurs to choose them: 'Charles Ross', perhaps,
instead of Cox for October/November; and brown-skinned,
white-fleshed 'Egremont Russet' instead of Ellison's for late
September.

Our winter apples, the hard apples we store in bags for
January and February and March, seem, unlike our summer
apples, disease resistant: we grow the old East Anglian collec-
tor's piece, 'D'Arcy Spice', bred in 1850, a greeny-brown russet
of spicy and distinctive flavour; and a modern apple, 'Winston',
hard, red, sweet, and an excellent keeper.

Apple trees demand care; you have to learn how to prune
them. I battle round the trees in the cold Christmas holidays,
hooded in my anorak, first with long-handled secateurs and an

2 a) **The orchard**: standard apples grow along the old herbaceous
border, and a new mixed border nods to it across the grass. The face of
the cottage is now half-hidden behind trees.

2 b) **The path to the cottage door**: two apple trees ('George Cave' and
'Worcester') and two Irish yews give traditional symmetry on either side
of the gravel path, and 'Zéphirine Drouhin' still produces a rose or two
round the door, though now the August border phlox are blooming with
the Japanese anemones above self-seeded *Alchemilla mollis*, artemisia
and spurge.

aluminium ladder, pruning ever more strictly as the years go by; then with pressure spray pack on my back, administering the lethal, white, tar-smelling fluid which is euphemistically called a 'winter wash', and which really does eliminate aphids, caterpillars and moths at the egg stage. I then throw reels of black nylon thread up and down amongst the bare branches in the hope of discouraging those gorgeous marauders in their apricot-tinted waistcoats, the bullfinches. In early May, I'm at it again, my plastic spray now filled with systemic fungicide in the hope of defeating scab, and if I can find the energy and conviction, I repeat the dose at 'petal fall'. It would be a comfort if my conscience told me not to use sprays; instead it tells me not to be lazy, and that I must work hard for a good apple harvest. And still our pippins and Worcesters have blotches on their cheeks, but our apple trees are a joy: a joy in blossom, and a joy in fruit; and all the year round, they soften the front face of our cottage; they have made it nestle down snugly behind leaves and branches and belong to its garden again.

Conversely, we have made the garden belong to the solid, timber-framed house, by planting three of those sturdiest of trees, Irish yews, across the front, one on either side of the gravel path, a few feet from the front door, and a third in line with them and marking the cottage's end. Perhaps we had seen pairs of Irish yews full-grown and architectural in front of old cottages whose gardens had not, like ours, disappeared. At any rate, we knew from the first that these very dark, very slow-growing, very old-fashioned trees would look right. All gardens need evergreens to give solidity in winter, but the fashionable answer of dwarf conifers seemed quite wrong, both modern and alien, in our cottage garden. Irish yew is as dark as ink. It assumes, as it grows, the most satisfying flutings, like the columns in a Gothic nave; it ends, not pointed at the top, but squared off, in a way which suits the horizontal roofbeam of a thatch; but it is never shaggy or untidy like its English counterpart; it has a solid neatness. To some people, it suggests churchyards and death;

to me it suggests security and immemorial years. Our yews must have been under three feet high when we planted them in 1965, but even then they had the substance which gave the west face of our cottage a sense of being at last anchored to the ground. In twenty years they have grown to about fifteen feet; I hope they will be allowed, by succeeding generations, to go on growing and slowly thickening for as long as the cottage itself stands.

The field on the east side of the house was a separate problem; here lay another northern boundary to be blotted out. We did not hesitate. We chose poplars; they perfectly reflected the feverishness of our desire for quick, tall growth, an emphatic protest against the flat landscape with its 'A' road. We planted twelve of them in our first autumn, barely 10 feet apart – six along the northern boundary, just inside the hedge, and six at right angles, down the eastern edge of the field, with a balsam poplar in the angle where the two lines joined. We knew that poplars sucker, but we did not care. We still do not regret them, and try not to mind as we yank the suckers out of the asparagus bed.

They have done what we asked of them; they have grown prodigiously; they are a pleasant landmark, now, from the main road; they are silver poplars, *Populus alba* 'Pyramidalis' – tall and slender as lombardy poplars, but in colour more sympathetically attuned to the grey-green bat willows at the bottom of the field. The balsam, *P. balsamifera*, is different, green and rounded, with more typical poplar leaves; it is said to be the quickest growing of all poplars, but ours is in fact dwarfed by its six tall silver sentinels on either side. But each spring I rejoice in it when I catch an unexpected whiff of balsam on the air; then I cut its sticky buds while they are still tight, and the exciting balsam scent fills the house; it lasts for weeks while the buds open into joyous bright green leaves which seem to fly from the stems like butterflies.

To relate our cottage to its garden and to blot out the northern

view was only half our aim in choosing trees; the other half was
to relate our garden to the surrounding fields and hedgerows.
The natural trees of the water meadows that lay to our south
were oak, ash, hawthorn and, above all, willow. And, since
speed of growth was still important to us, we wanted to plant
more willows.

At first, we longed for the most spectacular – the weeping
willow, so glorious when fully grown and rightly placed. We
had, as yet, no water for it to dangle its long fingers in, but the
dairy farm next door had an unsightly grey weatherboard shed
on our boundary which dominated our view to the west and
which we thought we could hide with a weeping willow tree.
One drizzling autumn day my husband stood disconsolately in
his macintosh in front of this shed while I peered at him through
the little sitting room window and waved him a little to the left
. . . a little to the right . . . until I judged that he stood in the
direct line of view between window and shed. (Somewhere I had
read this important tip: align your plantings to the views from
your windows.) Then he drove the marking stake into the earth
and there we planted our first weeping willow, to be followed,
the next spring, by a second one nearby. Alas, these willows
came from a nursery whose stock proved to be infected with that
dreaded fungus disease which was attacking weeping willows a
few years ago. Each spring their young twigs suffered die-back;
for years we went on hoping, we sprayed, we prayed, we
pruned; at last we acted blindly and boldly and sawed the two
poor ailing trees off at the ground.

Now I am glad we have not got those willows. They are
superb beside the Cam at Cambridge, glorious beside the canals
of French châteaux; less good, much less good, on the lawns of
suburban gardens; oversize and inappropriate in cottage gardens too. We have now, instead, a most beautiful, and indeed
spectacular specimen willow, *Salix alba sericea* 'Argentea'; it
has grown 30 feet in ten years and is a symmetrical pyramid in
shape. In this landscape of silvery willows it is, as its name

implies, the silveriest of all, silver as a scotch thistle or cotton lavender, and the lightness of its leaves means that, even in a gentle breeze, it is always shimmering. Not far away from it we have the smaller and more fashionable silver tree, the willow-leafed pear, *Pyrus salicifolia* 'Pendula', which weeps prettily in a corner while the silver willow reaches for the sky.

One of the bonuses of the whole family of willow trees is that, even in August when so many deciduous trees look dark, dull green, their leaves are light and fresh. But another bonus lies in their winter bark. And it was this which led us to the *alba* willows in the first place. Our garden in winter was dull, and we had read about the brilliance of *Salix alba* 'Britzensis' and the orange-red of its young stems. We planted a row of five of these red-twigged willows in front of one row of poplars. Each spring we cut them hard back to their central stem to encourage the new growth that is essential to coloured bark; after pruning they look like mutilated witches' brooms; but by midsummer they have burst forth again exuberantly with long, supple, leafy wands, and by the winter these wands are smooth, shining and red as sealing wax, a glory when they catch low rays from the winter sun, and a warming sight even on a sunless day.

For, as the years went by in our garden, we became greedy for beauty at all seasons. If there is something very soft and pretty in high summer about our silvery trees, in spring and autumn they contribute little. They cannot give fresh young green, since green is not to be their colour, and silver trees do not turn red in autumn, though the *alba* poplars do manage a brief, pale yellow. For autumn colour we relied at first upon our cherry trees (and only *Prunus sargentii* proved quite reliable) our hawthorns, our medlar with its late hanging, rich brown leaves, and a self-sown English oak which we have allowed to grow and flourish in the boundary hedge beside the lane; but we felt dismally short of red and russet in October, and we have now planted the tree which my husband thinks is the most beautiful English tree of all, though it is not specially East Anglian and is very far from cottagey – *Fagus sylvatica*, a forest beech. It is at the bottom of the lawn and so far it does not look wrong.

It has two first cousins to keep it company, a pair of Dawyck beeches, *Fagus* 'Fastigiata', the fastigiate beeches which are sometimes mistaken for lombardy poplars by the uninitiated, but which have the solidity, the shining beauty of foliage and the sheer breeding to which poplars cannot aspire. These two beeches have a special function in our garden; they stand on either side of a vista which we have now achieved across the water meadows – in other words, they mark each side of a wide gap we have cut in our southern hedge. Fastigiate trees are good at thus pinpointing and defining a vista, without masking it; besides, there is something extraordinarily satisfactory about a pair of slender trees, and the eye will rest upon them as well as looking between them to the view beyond. These trees hold their leaves until December, turning from russet to the warmest and spiciest of browns.

For winter, we wanted evergreens. The little Irish yews near the house were not enough; we longed to plant a cedar of Lebanon as a specimen on the south-sloping grass, a pledge to the future; having planted so many fast-growing trees, we could afford to redress the balance and plant a few very slow-growing ones, which would still be there long after the others had fallen. But none of the nurseries we consulted stocked cedars of Lebanon, and the only wide-spreading cedar they listed was *Cedrus atlantica* 'Glauca'; again, we thought, too modern, too showy, for our garden plan; silver was all right, but blue was not. In the end I contented myself with a container-grown *Cedrus deodara*, the pendulous cedar whose branches would look as though they were perpetually weighed down with heavy snow, were it not that they are bright moss green. But we did not like this tree enough to make it our lawn specimen, and it is now growing perhaps a little too near the western boundary hedge for its later comfort.

So what were our evergreen lawn specimens to be? I went to

Kew Gardens and I saw the avenue of holm oaks which are so magnificently spreading and shapely that few people could fail to admire them. Unaware of how paltry less fortunate holm oaks can look, we optimistically marked two widely spaced spots on our grass (after much careful squinting out of windows) and ordered two holm oaks, along with our other original trees, in the autumn of 1965. They arrived in pots, as they dislike transplanting; they were little pot-plants which could be measured in inches.

But they have grown. Pliny is said to have found *Quercus ilex* the most satisfying of trees, for at every stage of its long years of growth it is beautiful. After ten years, our plants ceased to look like fattening shrubs and became trees. Their circumference is perhaps rather greater than their height, but after a dozen years they were at least fourteen feet high and were landmarks to be reckoned with. Now, they have a sort of stateliness; they are solid and rounded from their tips right to the ground; no trunk can yet be seen. In colour they vary, from dull green in winter to silvery-ochre when the velvety new growths cover the whole domed tree in spring. Indeed, in these evergreens, we have unwittingly carried on the silver-grey colour scheme of so much of our planting, so that both in shape and in colour these ilexes probably harmonise better with their surroundings (remembering the rounded hedgerow oaks of the meadows below us) than any coniferous evergreens could have done.

We are not without conifers; we have a swamp cyprus, the slow-growing, bright green, deciduous conifer of which one sometimes sees superb mature specimens growing in parks. We also have two groups of Scots pines, *Pinus sylvestris*, growing at either end of our lines of poplars; they are still young enough to be roughly Christmas tree in shape, but infinitely softer in colour and foliage; one day their trunks will be bare, and their top branches will take interesting shapes against the sky.

For trees will take their own shapes; this is something to remember. You will never quite know how any chosen tree will look until it has grown, for each tree is individual, unpredictable. One of our holm oaks is shaplier, more symmetrical, than the other, which is struggling to catch up. Each of our Irish yews is subtly different. But all our trees are still young; the older they grow, the more formed, individual and distinctive they will become. It is a great day when you can remove the stake from a standard tree and see its own strong young trunk bear its weight. At that moment it first seems to achieve a balanced shape.

It is getting hard to remember how our initial planting looked – all those little leggy standards and half-standards, each fastened to its stake with a tree-tie, and none making any difference to the view at all. Our original order contained thirty-five trees and cost £30. It seemed, at the time, a bold extravagance. We nearly lost half of it in the first winter after planting, for we did not know that when you plant new trees in the country you must put a cylinder of wire netting round their stems to protect them from the rabbits who will otherwise chew their soft young bark. Many of our trees were chewed before the Christmas holidays, but fortunately none was chewed right round before we rescued them, and though some were sadly wounded, all recovered.

There was something else I did not know at first; you should keep a wide ring of ground round your newly-planted trees weed-free for several years, until the trees are well grown enough to have sent their roots out deep and wide. I let the couch grass creep to within ten inches of my poor trees, and they did not seem to grow very fast. Then I was advised to give each tree a bed of three feet wide all round it, a bed, in fact, which measured six feet across. I spent a week or more cutting turves away round every tree and mulching the bare ground with farmyard manure. I enjoyed myself, but now I suspect that spading the ground clean was wrong; apart from being unnecessarily strenuous, it was removing topsoil from the tree each time I did it – for in our couch-infested soil the job had to be redone each year – and gradually the planting level of the tree would be changed and even, perhaps, the point at which it was grafted might appear.

The answer is now obvious, if expensive; I must use paraquat each spring round all trees that grow in grass and cover the dying vegetation with a good mulch of anything that comes to hand, even cut grass or hay.

Planting trees on a virtually treeless site is the most important thing a gardener can do. Every autumn for at least six years after our first major planting, my husband insisted that we must plant more trees. We must have planted over fifty.

Now, at last, we have called a halt. We see a tulip tree going cheap at an open day at a stately garden. We are tempted, but where would we put it? It would not fit into any of our plans; we must say no. I long for a mulberry, but we have already fitted in enough such single fruit and nut trees. A walnut tree? A quince? We must say no. Sometimes, we dream of a pleached lime *allée* – but we know the dream is idiotic; there is nowhere to put it at all. We have done enough; the ugly view is blotted out, and shadows are beginning to lengthen across the lawn.

IV

The Climbers and the Tubs

There was another way in which we sought to marry our cottage to its site: we must clothe its staring white walls with plants. Here two things stood in our way: first, as so often in restored cottages, the builders had put a sloping shoulder of concrete right up to the foot of the walls in many places so that there was no room for a bed; second, the thatch jutted out solidly above in many places, like an umbrella warding off the rain. But there were five or six places where the concrete was not spread, and in some of these the thatch did not jut, so these were the prize spots.

The choice of climbers was governed by two very simple considerations: I wanted sweet flower scents to float in at the windows – jasmine, honeysuckle – and we wanted at least some things that would flower in July and August, when we had longest to enjoy them. A third, negative consideration was this: we did not want rampant climbing roses which would send mighty thorny canes up two storeys and into the thatch, needing that expert professional training, tying in and pruning, with vine eyes and wires along the walls, which we knew by experience we were inept at giving. The point is proved by the 'New Dawn' rambler which we planted against the shed and which is now rampaging all over it, knocking old pantiles off its roof, however murderously we cut it back each summer. A disappointment, this rose, as it does not provide the continuous or repeat-flowering we had hoped for, but gives all its roses in one abundant shell-pink shower in July, before we are here to enjoy it. Perhaps, though we had ordered the 'New Dawn', we were sent its elderly relation, 'Dr Van Fleet.'

Roses, when they are officially called climbers, can be over-poweringly rampant. On the other hand, roses are right for cottages, more right than anything else could ever be. Half the humble cottages of England were probably once called 'Rose Cottage'; ours was, we know, before the recent vendor suppressed this name. And so we succumbed to the notion of roses round the door, and we chose 'Zéphirine Drouhin' – first, because she is a repeat-flowerer, giving hope of roses in late summer; second, because she is not rampant, not strictly a climber at all, but a Bourbon shrub rose of modest strength which reacts well to being spread out like a fan against a wall; thirdly, because few roses smell more deliciously, headily sweet than she; and finally, of course, because she is the famous rose without a thorn. I do not include her colour in the list of her virtues because I have a love-hate relationship with it. If ever a rose was *rose pink* it is 'Zéphirine Drouhin' – that deep, deep, voluptuous pink which has no yellow in it at all and quite a hint of blue. In an unkind mood, one could call it puce. In a different mood, when showing visitors round the garden – visitors whom I suspect of liking the warm, sunset colours of the modern floribundas – I feel half-ashamed of Zéphirine blooming away intensely pink against the white walls by the door. If the walls themselves were washed a pale Suffolk pink or even ochre, I wonder if this might dilute her concentrated pink? And yet, in a more positive mood, or when a welcome visitor greets Zéphirine as an old friend, I love her whole-hearted, scented pinkness and would not change it. True, she has a propensity for mildew, but a spray or two with systemic fungicide early in the season keeps this at bay. Otherwise she behaves herself; she is just the right size; she goes, willingly, where you want her to go, vertically up beside the door, horizontally along under the windows, smothered in bloom in June, blooming again, with less abundance, in September, and usually supplying a few sprays of flowers in all the weeks between; an obedient, deservedly famous old rose.

We put our honeysuckle against a large space of windowless wall which needed clothing; it did the job quickly and thoroughly, climbing up a plastic-covered trellis, and in three or four years it had filled its allotted rectangle of space; it is easy to cut it back each year to its rightful proportions, either after flowering or at the beginning of the year, but important to remember; once, when we forgot, it became so bushy that it pulled its entire trellis off the wall. The smell is sweetest in the evening; we have trained it to reach our bedroom window-sill, and sometimes at night I swear that I have been woken up by sudden wafts of its scent, it is so strong. The flower buds are wine red, the flowers open pink and butter yellow; the berries are red; the leaves blue-green; even in winter, it looks bushy rather than bare; in a good season, it flowers from July to August for four or five lovely weeks. It has proved itself indispensable: *Lonicera periclymenum* 'Serotina', the late Dutch honeysuckle.

The scent of jasmine is shier; it seems not to hang on the air like honeysuckle's, perhaps because it is less profuse in flowering, nor is its season so long. It usually flowers in July and is over in three weeks. Ours is a pink form, *Jasminum × stephanense*; if you pick a sprig for a vase and bury your nose in it, nothing is more delicious. Otherwise, its little starry scented flowers, while sweet, are insignificant, though sudden wafts of scent may surprise you as you pass by. The plant itself, however, is by contrast highly significant; it grows with a vigour which seems impossible to discourage; we have used it to mask a fairly ugly little flat-roofed porch which had been added to our cottage in the angle of its 'L'; in a very few years, it not only achieved this job, but made a little porch itself – a solid, clipped eave of jasmine, a sort of living thatch above the back door and reaching upward to frame bedroom windows. Perhaps our jasmine grows particularly well because it has got its feet into the damp earth under some paving; or perhaps because it is in the sheltered corner of the L-shaped cottage facing south; or perhaps it is always vigorous. I have seen it like this, clipped, neat and bushy round the doors of other cottages in real life and in photographs. Its foliage is almost as starry and insubstantial as its flowers; it comes late, and hangs on late. When the leaves burst, they are a surprising mixture of primrose and pink; they settle down to a fresh green. You can make a frame of it round a window, and what you lose in light you gain in the enchantment of looking out onto a garden through a soft wreath of green.

Our third scented climber is wisteria. My mind had long been haunted by this line of Henry Newbolt's:

'The wisteria trailing in at the open window . . .'

so, though it blooms in May and not in August, I was determined it should trail in through our biggest window, open to welcome it in May. I still await those long, mauve racemes along the window-sill; other people's wisterias start to bloom when they are still young; ours only achieves a few flowers and concentrates, each spring, on leaf. I suspect that birds peck off the buds in winter. The only comfort is that the young, soft, lime-beige leaves of wisteria are outstandingly beautiful amongst the greens of spring – though doubly so when seen as a subtly shaded foil to the mauve flowers. You have to be bossy with climbing plants, and particularly with wisteria; all summer long it will throw out yards of tendrils in the wrong direction as soon as your back is turned – under the tiles or up into the air, and you must be continually ready to prune it or twist it in another direction, the direction you want it to take. The more it is pruned, we tell ourselves, the more likely it is to flower next year. We are gradually persuading it to follow a horizontal course, all round the tiled lean-to at the southern end of the cottage. Its main prunings come in July and again in October or November. There is pleasure in finding, one day, that the twisted tendrils have become a strong, twisted grey trunk, and that the wilful wisteria has made itself into an architectural adjunct to the house.

In a narrow bed which exists between a path and the wall, round the corner from the wisteria, we planted the familiar 'japonica', *Chaenomeles superba* 'Rowallane', a variety with extra large, sealing-wax blooms. It is not allowed to grow outwards, strictly upwards and sideways – the secateurs see to that when flowering finally ceases in June. This year, it is acting as a perfect climbing frame for clematis 'Comtesse de Bouchard', which has covered it since its own flowering ended and has made that space against the white wall, so recently trimmed with scarlet, a solid wall of pink. I shall cut the clematis right down in winter. It remains to be seen whether the chaenomeles will recover from the deprivation of summer light and give its full performance again next year.

Certainly, for adorning cottage walls in July and August, the most obvious and triumphant answer is clematis – the large-flowered Jackmanii varieties which bloom on the new wood for about six resplendent weeks. The special value of these clematis lies partly in the fact that they are *not* architectural permanencies demanding skilful training; they are ephemeral glories of the summer, all bud and flower and powder-puff seed head for two months, and then – gone until next year. No skill at all is needed in assisting this cycle of dormancy and flower; all that is needed is five minutes, in February, with sharp secateurs. I bought my clematis from the noted East Anglian hybridiser, J. Fisk of Westleton, and read, and conscientiously followed, his published instructions in his book *Success with Clematis*. This meant that in the first year I had to be ruthless; I pruned all my clematis back at least three times in their first spring, cutting the new growth and so persuading two strong shoots to come from each cut, instead of the single tendril that would otherwise have grown thinly up the wall. After the first year each plant had developed multi-stemmed framework and was ready to spread out and clothe its space in an obedient fan. In successive Februaries I cut each plant almost down to the old wood, just as the sap is beginning to rise, and scatter a handful of sulphate of potash round the roots, covering it with a cosy mulch of manure. I then rather half-heartedly attempt to pull the old dead stems with their little hooked brown clingers off the white clematis 'netlon' – but if the February wind is strong and it is too cold and dispiriting to finish this job, I leave it, knowing that before many weeks the new green growth will be hiding the old.

We started with two large-flowered hybrids, a pink and a blue, both famous favourites. The pink was the 'Comtesse de Bouchard' mentioned above, lilac pink with rounded sepals; the blue was 'Perle d'Azur', its sepals also rounded and its blue a lilac blue. The pink is always the first to bloom, usually starting before June is out; in a good year, they each still have a flower or two in September. They are required, by me, to spread out wide rather than to grow high, and they cover about a ten foot span. They both put up with a largely easterly aspect, and look lovely planted side by side.

It is fun teaching a clematis where it is to go; if you are very deft, you can unwind its little clinging leaf stems (which always wind themselves onto their support in the opposite direction from that which you expect), and wind them on elsewhere, though at first, in their new position, they will hold like a loose handshake. It is worth taking this trouble with clematis, and it carries a finicky fascination, rather like doodling. If you leave the clematis to its own ideas, it will rise in a narrow pillar of tangled stems all clinging to each other and the flowers will be so closely bunched that half their glory will be unseen.

In later years we have added three more large-flowered hybrids to our collection: a red, designed to scramble through the honeysuckle and prolong its flowering season into late August; it is called 'Mme Edouard André', and its colour, like that of all the coloured hybrids, has not quite forgotten its mauve-purple origins, and is a dull crushed raspberry. (It is pretty, but confused, for it blooms at the same time as the honeysuckle by mistake; by happy chance, its red mirrors the honeysuckle's red buds.) Then we have 'Victoria', much the largest flowered and most spectacular of our clematis, intense blue-mauve, with five pointed sepals; she climbs through the 'New Dawn' rose and half-way along a nearby hedge and is still floriferous in September, perhaps because she's altered her aspect and now faces south; and finally, we have added the first and most famous of them all, the original old purple Jackmanii, which has decorated cottage walls since it first flowered over a hundred years ago. Once, in its second year, this clematis nearly died of wilt – the only case of clematis wilt that we have yet encountered. Grim and pessimistic, but obedient to the book, we immediately cut it to the ground. It revived and now, four years later, it is climbing half-way up our eastern chimney in a wide column of large purple flowers; in its mixture of strength and beauty it is still a winner.

There are, of course, other brands of fool-proof clematis – fool-proof because they require no pruning at all. There is the popular *C. montana*, the rampant small-flowered white or pink clematis of May. Ours is the pink, *C. montana* 'Rubra'; it covers the whole northern gable of our cottage and its ambition is to cover the whole thatch as well. So after all it must be pruned; an extension ladder must be mounted and it must be slashed back every June after flowering.

We have fitted in other spring-flowering species: *C. alpina*, of modest dimensions and sweet, dangling blue flowers; it needs no pruning and flowers in April but this makes its blooms susceptible to frost; and, lovelier still, *C. macropetala*, whose dangling flowers are frilled and double, like a ballet dancer's skirts, with paler petticoats peeping beneath the outside sepals' blue. I tried this especially beloved clematis in a tub placed where concrete met the cottage walls; it was beautiful when it flowered, but after a few years it died – a single *non*-'success with clematis'.

But tubs are obviously the answer to concrete screeds. I bought ours at local auction sales – large, sawn-in-half barrels, and added a fine Italian pottery olive vase which I saw on a pavement outside an Ipswich junk shop. The vase came to rest immediately on the concrete slab that marked the septic tank, in nice view of the kitchen window – rather too grand at first, a formal vase in a field of tussocks; it was a long time before we discovered the plant that would look right growing in it; it needed something that would trail down its graceful rounded flanks, and not spring upwards like a chimney sweeper's brush through its narrow mouth; it must also be something that would survive neglect and lack of regular water. In the end the common variegated periwinkle, *Vinca major* 'Variegata', has settled there; it can't spread far, which must displease it though it pleases us, but it does spread down the sides, and even when neglected it is difficult to kill. I suppose a variegated small-leafed ivy would have been more graceful, except that it might have clung to, and obscured, the vase's sides.

In theory you can grow almost anything in a tub if you water it and feed it, even an apple tree; in practice, some shrubs are much more amenable than others. Everyone knows that camellias and the smaller rhododendrons and azaleas, with their compact root balls, do well in tubs; but they belong to a family which looks foreign here. Bay trees, too, are classic container plants, but less than ideal in biting East Anglian winter winds; nevertheless we are nurturing a little bay tree, erecting a wind-screen round it in the winter.

There was a spot on the north side of the cottage, right on the lane, where the occasional car passing through a puddle on a rainy day splashed the white wall. A tubbed evergreen was needed, dense and strong, to ward off the mud. I chose a pyracantha, *Pyracantha rogersiana*, because it has a wonderfully strong pattern of vertical and horizontal branches and can rival an espaliered fruit tree against a house wall. The poor, strong-growing thing must have longed to escape its tub and let its roots go free, but even in its straitened circumstances it lived and spread quite wide, until it died in a vicious frost one spring. I have replaced it with a winter jasmine; its gentle, arching growths agree to be trained conveniently to cover dirty patches on the wall, and it flowers courageously whenever winter weather allows.

Nearby it in summer stand fuchsias in pots: the hardy fuchsia 'Versicolor', whose grey-green/pink/cream leaves are more important than its small red flowers, and 'Thalia', with handsome russet leaves touched with dull green, and orange-red tubular flowers in pendant clusters. In winter 'Thalia' is moved indoors, to take her chance with life and death in a cold dry bedroom.

Meanwhile, potted tulips are starting into life. Tulips look handsome massed in big flower pots, safe from the fiery disease of scorched leaf-edges and wilting, stunted flowers which now ravages them in our garden soil. They still run the risk of attack by mice or sparrows who quickly discover the succulent bulbs in the loose compost a few inches below the surface, but fine wire netting stretched over them in winter keeps them safe. In April, they can be moved into the sun, and moved right out of sight again when flowering is done, until they have died down and are ready for lifting. Then the potting soil can be changed, as a further precaution against 'tulip fire'. If mice have discovered the bulbs in their dark cupboard and demolished them all before November's planting time comes round, it is an excuse to buy new bulbs, five for each pot. To choose new colours, new classes of tulips, is one of the best spectator sports at spring flower shows. The romantic tatters of the striped and feathered parrot tulips are perhaps too untidy and undulating for pots, and some of the Darwins are too tall; the straight conventional soldiers, the early singles and cottage tulips, are the best. I love the plump-flowered 'Apricot Beauty'; I love 'Sorbet', cool blush-white touched with rose; I particularly love the old 'Queen of Night', especially if mixed with the lily-flowered 'White Triumphator': the black and white colour scheme may sound too sophisticated for a country cottage, but proves otherwise.

In another barrel I grow two plants of *Dicentra spectabilis*, the 'Bleeding Heart', as sentimental as its name; the exquisite red and white lockets of this fragile but cottagey plant are half lost when dangling their heart-shaped pendants over the garden soil; lifted knee-high in a tub, and arching out over its rim, they catch the admiring eye as they should. And as they stand outside the kitchen door, I give them all the water that I can.

Right beside this door there is a rain-water down-pipe, disgorging onto the concrete slab below. It needed an amenable, not over-vigorous but fairly bushy climber to clothe it, or alternatively a slender upright shrub or towering herb – in each case something that would be happy in a pot. There was a succession of experiments and failures. Finally I stumbled on an answer: the everlasting pea, *Lathyrus latifolius*, a traditional old cottage plant with pink or cream pea flowers on long stems. In a fit of sentiment, I had raised a row of them from seed, and was looking for homes for the few survivors. I put one in a pot; it produced many stems, happy to embrace the pipe's circumference. It also grew upwards, all pea leaves and tendrils, in a cheerful bunch, tied together with raffia, robust and biddable.

Pots and tubs are versatile. They happily accommodate bulbs and annuals, fuschias and taller shrubs, weepers and climbers; but they also, in their man-made formality, provide a happy foil to little standard plants. We are training a pair of standard honeysuckles inspired by the group of four in the centre of the herb garden at Cranborne Manor in Dorset. We have untwisted two ordinary honeysuckle plants from their stakes, deprived them of their pairs of leaves for three feet of their length and re-staked them, very firm and straight, with the help of many ties. They are to shower out into rounded bouquets of honeysuckle at the tops of their standard stems, scenting the air before our 'Late Dutch' climber comes into flower. They stand symmetrically on a bit of paving, and we await developments, watering whenever they feel dry.

For watering is the problem with tubbed and potted plants at a weekend cottage in a dry part of England. I am amazed that our things survive at all. Often in summer we arrive on a warm weekend to find our tubbed hydrangea drooping, but one of the most satisfactory sights in a garden is to observe a hydrangea perking up again after it has had a can of water; you can almost see its tired leaves freshening. So we still have not lost our hydrangea – and, as its name suggests, it is a precious one: *H. acuminata* × 'Preziosa', a desirable thing whose comparatively small flowers combine rose pink with white, deepening with age to a tawny old-rose colour, and whose leaves change from grass green to red; the stems are red and seem to influence the colour of the leaves; but like most hydrangeas, it manages its shade mutations subtly, and its flowers last from July until the frosts. I have taken to emptying the tea-pot into its tub since it, too, stands conveniently near the kitchen door, and recently I have tipped the basin in which I scrub and peel potatoes into its tub as well. It has never looked better, but perhaps next year young potatoes will be sprouting round it.

I have left until the end the plant which rises to the problem of the unwatered tub, nay thrives upon it; the beautiful plant which flowers in July and right on through August to September and adorns whatever terrace it is placed on – the plant which has now learnt to survive the frosts of an English winter and which therefore gets my gold medal for the best tub-plant in ten years; it is the agapanthus – not the overblown, coarse old thing with giant round heads which grew like a weed in the sunny seaside gardens of my native Australia, but the delicate umbel of little blue trumpets, blue as willow pattern china, dancing gracefully on slender stems that never need staking: *A. campanulatus* 'Profusion', rightly named, for eight or ten tall stems, each with its own showy flower head, rise, when the plant is established, from a twelve-inch pot. The newer varieties 'Bressingham Blue' or 'Bressingham White' appear to be equally good. Agapanthus are specially good in pots, free-standing, for then you can see all round them. In winter they are gone – even their plentiful strap-like leaves, like the leaves of daffodils, have shrivelled and nothing but assorted weeds can be seen on the surface of the potting soil – but every May, the green tips of their leaves start pushing up again and by August they are prize-winners.

In our first summer here we had bought two inappropriate little white-painted wooden plant-holders as a bit of swank – the sort that are called Versailles tubs. Rather stingily, I bought one leggy, pink pelargonium for each; they would lean, in semi-overbalanced flower pots, inside the wooden boxes as we tried them in various places, outside the back door, then the front; we were trying to make our wasteland look a garden, and they were the only flowers we had. It took more than two pink geraniums to do the trick, and the Versailles tubs are now broken up in the garden shed.

But since then we have often returned to geraniums in summer and are seldom without a scented-leaved geranium in a pot. And this year we have two small half-barrel tubs outside the front door again and in them, for the first time, we have some pelargoniums which look right. The tubs are greyish, weathered-tub colour. The geraniums are white, chalk white, and perhaps they look so at home because they match the cottage walls – those bits that can still be seen between the creepers.

V

The Herbaceous Border

The story of this garden is for me, first, last and always, the story of its herbaceous border. That first summer, as soon as a path was cut through the weeds towards the dull yellow flowerheads which now marked the spot, I walked to the site and began my excavations. They took over two years – two years in which to determine, roughly, what the extent and composition of that boasted 'well-planned' border must have been. It was, indeed, excavation work, and in my own field I must have experienced the sustained excitement, hope and fatigue of an archaeologist.

'It's all *there* . . .' they had said, pointing through the window. It was not all there by August, and I shall never know quite what was lost. But, knitted with weeds, darned with their roots, woven with their over-arching stems, a number of robust plants survived, and the following spring the shoots of more brave clumps surfaced and could be spotted before the competition from weeds became too strong.

The yellow I had seen in May must have been a day lily; those early-flowering day lilies in their thickly matted clump of roots, almost a yard square, have resisted weeds entirely until this day; I have never lifted them; I wish I knew their name. They have a heavenly scent and are perfectly behaved.

The bright blue we saw in June must have been anchusa. It came, and went, but now is here to stay, for though each plant is short-lived, it is a self-seeder and I can collect the far-flung seedlings and return them to their appointed spot each year. Nothing is as blue as blue anchusa; the furry old stems are not attractive, but all is forgiven for the sake of the giant forget-me-not flowers, as blue as the Mediterranean sea. And during the droughts which anchusa loves, they are bluer than ever.

The yellow I followed in August proved to be *Achillea*

filipendulina 'Gold Plate', rising stiff and undaunted amongst the thistles, its flat head of gold as dry, wiry and determined as any weed. That clump of achillea was my talisman in 1965, and I have only to bend one of its stiff stems to my nose today to remember, in its aromatic, almost apple scent all the sensations and the toil of that first summer.

While my husband was straining along behind the Hayterette, and the air was full of its quick-firing noise, I was crouched, almost immobile, and usually invisible, amongst the tall weeds in the place where I took the herbaceous border to be. I had bought a small border fork, and a heavy iron workman's barrow, which stood a few yards away where we thought the 'lawn' was. My head was down, studying the vegetation. I tried not to move my feet, in case I stood on something that turned out to be precious. My horticultural knowledge was very limited. I had been through a brief phase of fanatical interest in our small strip of London garden before our children were born; at that time, I had joined the Royal Horticultural Society, attended their fortnightly shows, and visited Kew and Wisley, notebook in hand, writing down the names of plants that I thought would look nice in a London terrace strip. I had also worked along the two gardening shelves of our local public library, devouring books about other people's gardens. But I knew almost nothing about herbaceous plants; I certainly did not know that the approved way of dealing with a problem like mine would be to lift all the clumps of hardy perennials that could be identified and heel them in elsewhere in some rapidly cleared transit camp, then treat the whole area with weedkiller and wait until it was absolutely clean before putting the plants back again. I worked the other way round, lifting the weeds, leaving the plants. I started by forking out the weeds I recognised: thistles, nettles, docks, grasses, clover, dandelions, elder seedlings; I hurled them through the air into the waiting barrow. Anything I did not recognise, I left. Gradually I discovered groups of plants, groups with interesting and distinct leaves. I took them to be hardy

The rediscovered herbaceous border.

perennials, and would carefully excavate round them. I would get them roughly clear, though most of them would still be interwoven with couch. I suppose in this way I cleared about a third of the border, that first summer.

Two springs later, I found the boldness to lift some of the plants and start 'operating' upon them; I began with the achillea; I dug it all up, and sat with each clump upside down in my lap digging a sharp trowel into it and pulling out the hated white roots of couch grass which wove through its own fibrous roots like the warp of a doormat. I would sometimes have to break the clumps into little bits to reveal, and trace, those alien roots. Then I would replant the surviving pieces and see, with indescribable satisfaction, the little feathery achillea leaves sitting comfortably in the soil apparently free of couch. Not really free: I always missed bits and so, next year, I would have to 'operate' again. To the supposed joys of the archaeologist I thus add the supposed joys of the surgeon, in attempting to describe the complex experience of pleasure I had in rescuing that border.

It was at least a year before we could discover what shape the border was meant to be; in the end, we decided it had originally been kidney-shaped, though we were never certain. At any rate, it was very big: about seventeen paces long and five wide, running east and west, and thus facing south along its length. The famous local nursery of which the previous owner had boasted turned out to be Bressingham Gardens; we had thus unknowingly inherited a border planned by the acknowledged master of hardy perennials, an archetypal 'island bed' designed by the apostle of 'island beds', Alan Bloom, and planted by Adrian Bloom, his son; and like all archetypes, it survived neglect, an astonishing testimonial to the resilience of properly planted hardy perennials. We were indeed fortunate that underneath our waste land there lay this horticultural gift; at the very least, it gave us something to start from; it gave me the enormous pleasure of discovery, of reclamation, which is at least as exciting as planning one's own garden from scratch; in addition, of course, it gave us a superbly selected nucleus of the best strains of hardy plants, plants that lived amongst the greedy weeds from the time of their planting until I arrived on the scene with my fork some years later – for I am certain that the previous owners who had commissioned the bed had never weeded it at all. They had never lived here, and they were not gardeners. Perhaps, when placing their order, they had specified particularly 'hardy' hardy plants. Here, now, is a list of the survivors as a rollcall might have presented them two years after I started rescue work, when the excavating was more or less complete.

Beside the clumps of achillea were clumps of *Artemisia lactiflora*, a plant which will apparently survive all but extreme dryness, and whose tall, feathery cream flower-heads delight us in August to this day. Nearby was an early-flowering dark blue monkshood, and near it an apparently indestructible patch of a very pretty golden rod (solidago) budding lime green in late July, and blossoming gold in August and September. There was a patch of the tall yellow daisy of late summer, *Heliopsis scabra* 'Golden Plume', and a patch of doronicums, the short yellow daisies of early spring; there was a large clump of a beautiful blue *Iris sibirica*, with strong growing stems, frail flowers, now with many progeny throughout this garden and blooming abundantly in May; patches of a scented purple bergamot (monarda) appeared after a year's clearing to adorn the August border; a few bits of veronica, tall spikes of smoke blue; mounds of cranesbill, the perennial geranium, with very pretty leaves as well as large lavender-blue flowers in May, and beside it, equally rounded mounds of the perennial cornflower (catananche), with still more beautiful silvery leaves as finely cut as an acanthus, but fiercely magenta cornflowers. There were little ragged clumps of spiderwort (tradescantia) with pale blue-white trefoil flowers, the colour of skimmed milk, and, final surprise, after at least two years, there suddenly appeared a luscious rose-red lupin, evidently a seedling from former glories. All these plants, or their descendants, survive and flourish in the garden today.

And from them I gained the grand idea which I could never have formed without them: it was the concept of scale, the idea that for a herbaceous border to work at all, each species must occupy roughly a square yard, which means, in most cases, one must have three to five of any plant before moving on to the next one. As with trees, so with herbaceous plants; I would have bought one of a kind if I had not had the remains of a living example of how the thing ought to be done before my eyes. It hurts; it feels impossibly extravagant; but in those days there was an encouraging price reduction for anyone ordering three of a kind, and if I often ordered three where six were really needed, at least in many cases the plants would multiply or need dividing and in the end I could achieve the necessary six. Never in my wildest plans would I have conceived a border on this scale, but the remains of the thing were there, and I tried to continue as the professionals had begun.

For several years, 'doing' my herbaceous border was the main, and often-repeated task of my gardening holidays, the goal towards which I worked. The time it took to 'do' has gradually lessened; originally it would occupy almost an entire holiday; later, one week in spring to work from end to end; then, as the weeds became discouraged, perhaps three days, and now, if things go right, it may take only two; that is, two days in spring, from end to end; two or three days in autumn, from end to end, and periodic light cultivation in between. 'Doing' the herbaceous border does *not* mean staking; that, thanks to Alan Bloom's notion of hardy plants in an island bed, is something that never happens in my border. The plants grow freely and strongly, light and air on all sides of them, standing up and blowing in the breeze as they would stand and blow in a field, for they are all only the rich relations of meadow flowers – pretty, cultivated weeds; that's why they look right here. The weeds that grew originally all over our piece of land did not need staking; they staked each other. So, from end to end of my border, there is not a stake; the occasional stem flops, but that looks better than the occasional stake would do. 'Doing' the border means, rather, weeding – and weeding, for many years, has meant one accursed thing: my struggle with couch grass. I suppose it comes in from the edges, those rough so-called lawns of ours. Its coarse green blades come up through the crowns of herbaceous plants, its white and buff jointed roots spread through the soil, along and down, horizontally and vertically, indefinitely. But there is one nice thing about weeding couch: when you get a firm hold of a good bit of root, and start to ease it out with a trowel, with any luck it does not break; often you have the supreme satisfaction of feeling you have eradicated a whole network of couch grass roots at a scoop.

Not so with bindweed. I used to think that, when I died, 'couch grass' would be graven on my heart. Now I know the word will be 'bindweed'. For couch grass and I seem, after twelve years' battle, to have reached a truce; or rather I think at last I may be winning, partly because I am now fairly fussy about regularly cutting the edges of the lawn all round the border with my sharp edging shears. But the bindweed only arrived in the border three years ago, in a load of manure, I fear, and each year it is getting worse. Soon there will be a system of stakes in my proud, free-standing border after all: the plants will be laced and tied with bindweed; the revolting, insidious thing not only barley-sugars its way up any stem it finds, its roots are twisty too, twirling round like evil white springs in the earth. And when you catch hold of them and pull, they just break off in your hand; they look juicy but they are brittle; what is more, they go on for ever, circling down, down below the soil as, above ground, they spiral up and up. If you can chase them down with a long sharp trowel for six inches or more, you may reach the point of junction where the consistency of the root changes, from juicy to woody, and the colour changes from white to buff. I have tried, encouraged by gardening journalists, dangling the green growths into old jam jars full of a weak solution of weedkiller; no good, and how ridiculous the jam jars look, punctuating the border. I have tried dabbing with spot-on sticks of weedkiller, smearing it on the leaves; not much good, though possibly worth pursuing. I have not yet dared to dig down, as I have been recommended, and pour a weak solution of weed-killer into the hole by the root. I am working on the principle that every time I see a bit of bindweed, whether I have my trowel with me or not, I just pull it, break if off at ground level. Surely if it were never allowed to grow above ground, broken off each time it showed its head, it might die in the end?

For years 'doing the herbaceous border' has meant forking all through it with my border fork, and throwing all the weeds and waste into the wheel barrow and carting it away. I have carted mountains. But our soil is very light and sandy, and to cart away the rubbish all the time must impoverish the soil. Hardy perennials are not especially greedy, but East Anglian springs and summers are the driest in England, and humus is the need. I aim now, after the spring 'doing' of the border, to mulch the whole surface with something; once or twice it has been farmyard manure; last year it was old thatch; this year it was straw; next year it may be compost. The more I can mulch it, the less 'doing' it will need, for the mulch suppresses weeds.

It is a very big border now. We decided it should be straight, for traditional straight lines accorded with our image of an old-fashioned garden as more naturalistic curves and kidney shapes did not. We were not pursuing naturalism or romantic flowing lines – we were after a sort of unfussy formality which might give a sense of order and of peace. So we drew a long straight line where we thought the border's edge should be, and we extended that line a bit in the direction of the house so that it would not seem quite such an isolated incident as it did. We ended with a bed nineteen paces long and five paces wide. In winter it is nothing much – a collection of brown stems – but in summer it is the dominating feature of the garden.

The true herbaceous border, one that dies away in winter and reappears in spring, is not fashionable any more. The trend is

still firmly towards the mixed border, one in which hardy
perennials mingle with bulbs, roses and shrubs. It is said herbaceous plants are a nuisance because, so it's claimed, they need
staking and dividing, and are a dead loss in winter. I take the
point, but all gardening is a nuisance unless you like it, and most
bits of the garden look fairly dead in winter. I enjoy sharp
seasonal contrasts: the dying year, the metamorphosis of spring;
I also enjoy dividing plants; cutting them in half with a sharp
spade is a crude, instant method of propagation which I find
much easier than the taking of cuttings. In fact, I do very little
dividing – perhaps three or four different groups a year; some of
my plants have never been divided. I did, at first, make some
feeble gestures in the direction of the mixed border; someone
gave me four creamy pink floribunda roses, 'Sweet Repose', and
I stuck them at intervals down the border. I added some lilies,
tiger lilies and madonnas, and parrot tulips for the spring. But
they did not look right, marooned in the long island bed
amongst those masses of what Russell Page calls 'coloured hay'.
My border flowers are light and ephemeral as long summer
grasses and crops of grain; that is their charm. They do not need
to be given body; the roses and lilies and tulips, luscious flowers
of great intrinsic beauty, do not belong amongst them and look
better, now, elsewhere.

There are a few sub-shrubby things which, for one reason or
another, pass muster amongst my border flowers; shrubby
potentillas, lemon yellow and white, are useful at the border's
edge, for they flower all over, right down to the ground; some
dwarf bushes of bright blue hyssop are all right, too. At the far
end of the border, the architectural and bushy *Euphorbia
wulfenii* gives definition, both when its original, budgerigar-
coloured flowers rise in flat-topped umbels into the air, and
when its lovely foliage stands, freshly glaucous, against the
autumn brown of a hornbeam hedge; two plants of the pink
flowered shrubby mallow, lavatera, are invaluable; I often treat
them like herbaceous plants anyway, especially after a hard

winter, and cut them down in spring. The shrubby blue perovskia, or Russian sage, responds best to being cut down like a
herbaceous plant in spring as well. And so, in the winter, almost
everything in the border looks dead. But I follow the advice of
William Robinson, the famous Victorian gardener, and leave
them standing in their shades of brown until the spring. They
give a sort of quiet winter furnishing to their part of the garden,
and look better than a neatly cut-down, two-dimensional,
virtually empty bed of wet brown soil would do. I only cut them
down when there is the excitement of the little humps and tufts
of new growth starting. From then on, the border is a fluid,
ever-changing delight, gradually growing, taller, fuller, altering
its proportions and patterns of shapes until it reaches its full
stateliness of height and contrast in July and August. Change is
part of the essence of a garden, for it is allied to life, and growth;
the yearly metamorphosis of the herbaceous border is its most
pronounced example.

For us, of course, another attraction of herbaceous plants was
their flowering season; the herbaceous border reaches its peak in
August, the summer holiday month. For our border does not
contain the giant, June-flowering beauties; delphiniums and
peonies and the tall hybrid German irises which all need staking.
Three quarters of the plants in ours bloom when midsummer is
past. We did not ask of our border that it should be equally
interesting from May to September. We were content with a few
hints, a few promises in the spring and early summer: hints from
some of those brave survivors that were already there: the gold
doronicums with their big, simple daisy flowers in April; the day
lilies and irises in May; in June the showy lupins and the blue
cranesbill and anchusa and catmint (*Nepeta mussinii*); we were
grateful for their presences. But almost everything we added
ourselves flowered later: it suited us to have a spectacular border
for two months rather than a patchily flowered one for five. (In
fact, we have our cake and eat it; the border is patchily flowered
for three months and spectacular for two.)

This principle of concentrating one's planting upon August might well be applied to more than the holiday cottage garden; whoever spoke of a 'June gap' was eccentric; it is the August gap that threatens English gardens. Until July, a garden progresses under its own steam; nothing need be done about it; lovely effects are likely to be there; spectacle follows spectacle and there is always a feeling of expectancy – of growth towards some future climax. Unless one deliberately plants for August, no climax will come; the garden will suddenly have gone dull and sad and *over*.

In choosing plants that flowered in July and August that I liked, all I had to do was stroll round the famous six acre display gardens at Bressingham, catalogue and pencil in hand, and pick my pets. I was on my guard against yellow; after impulsively buying those little shrubs of tempting yellow potentilla at the outset, I suddenly realised that yellow threatened to engulf the whole border – the achillea, the helianthus and the golden rod were dominant; I was on the look-out for things to counteract the yellows – not scarlets and not crimsons which I find difficult to blend, but pinks, mauves, purples, whites and blues.

My July/August blues are these: the sea holly, eryngium, not the showy one with metallic stems and the odd huge head, but the smaller-flowered but much more generous one, widely branching *Eryngium tripartitum*; it has not been very long lived with me, but is almost indispensable and so I have replaced it when it has faded out; it is about two feet tall in my border, and

3 a) **Yew hedges**: bastions of yew lead the eye down towards the wood, past the Italian terracotta vase, a medlar and cherries (left) and the rounded shape of a holm oak half-visible on the right.

3 b) **The herbaceous border**: here are the rich relations of meadow flowers, tight-packed and unstaked. The blue globes of *Echinops ritro* tower over the flat gold heads of *Achillea filipendulina* 'Gold Plate'. The golden rod, *Solidago*, is still in its choice lime green stage, and an architectural *Yucca filamentosa* marks the corner.

its flower-heads are like lots of little mist-blue thimbles growing out of a stiff, starry ruff of sepals. It looks lovely with yellow (all blues do, perhaps) and even three plants of it will make a show. Next, the stately globe thistle, *Echinops ritro*, beloved of bees, six feet high and a spreader, like all thistles. Its flowers do not last nearly long enough and are a tedious brown when faded (they seem to last longer when picked for a vase) but at their peak they are so valuable in shape and colour that I can only thin them severely, never part with them; nothing else could compliment *Achillea filipendulina* 'Gold Plate' so well in colour and in shape: round blue globes rising a little higher than flat gold discs. (See Plate 3b.) Then there is the sky blue flax, *Linum narbonense*, which flowers profusely in June and July but is still going in August if the summer is sunny. It looks a fragile thing with its wiry arching stems, not very tall, and its shape is nothing when it is not in flower; but then, whenever one notices it, it is in flower, making all other blues look less than pure. A blue that shades to mauve is Russian sage, perovskia, the shrublet I have already mentioned; it is reminiscent of catmint with its long spikes of flowers and complementary little grey leaves, but taller, stiffer branching, more important and a better colour, and at its best in August. Another August winner is an aster, *A. thomsonii* 'Nana', a perfectly behaved little front-of-border plant, ten inches high and smothered in blue-mauve aster flowers with yellow centres for six weeks without fading or failing. There were liberal plantings of Michaelmas daisies in the original border, but all inextricably laced with couch grass; I vainly tried to rescue them, and achieved one brief show of flowers; but

4 **The August border**: pink, blue and silver cool the dominant yellows. The pinks come from the cone flower, *Echinacea purpurea* 'Robert Bloom', *Lavatera rosea* and *Anemone japonica* 'September Charm'; the blue is *Eryngium tripartitum* and the silver, *Anaphalis yedoensis*. Beyond the border you catch a glimpse of the three-tiered yew hedge leading to the willow (*Salix alba sericea* 'Argentea') and of a newly planted mulberry, a pledge to the future, on the lawn.

they succumbed to mildew and were too demanding; they go leafless and leggy at the bottom unless continually divided and re-planted; I decided they were more trouble than they were worth. *Aster thomsonii* 'Nana' is no trouble at all; it does not need to be divided, though you can divide it if, as will certainly happen, you want more of it; it does not get mildew and is worth all the others, except *Aster × frikartii*. This famous, long-lasting flower, two foot tall, is a priceless star of the late summer border. *Aconitum napellus* 'Bressingham Spire' is as blue as the monkshood I found in the border but blooms two months later, in August instead of June; it is so dark it is almost navy blue or purple; one thinks of it as tall, but it isn't. It looks well at the front of the border, its spires contrasting with more typically front-of-border things, though mine does not flower very generously nor for very long in dry years; what it wants is water.

I have bought only one true purple to add to the purple bergamot already in the border, and that is *Salvia × superba* 'May Night' which, as its name implies, starts to flower in May and, again true to its name, is superbly purple, a low solid block of colour at the front of the border for about five weeks. But later on it is a disappointment, though said to be a repeat flowerer; by July and August, despite careful deadheading, the main show is over, and there are only isolated and half-hearted spikes.

I had another purple flower, as tall as the salvia is small and as airy as it is dense: *Thalictrum dipterocarpum* 'Hewitt's Double', five feet tall, lacy like gypsophila, but larger and lovelier. It is a tricky thing, slow to increase, quick to die. I kept it for three years and moved it about from one richly manured spot to another as it is said to be restless and to like change; but it also likes moisture, and after the drought of 1976 it disappeared. I think its beauty is too fragile for the border; I shall try it elsewhere where it can be admired at close quarters and alone.

My most hard-working pink is the coarse old shrubby thing already mentioned, the tree mallow, *Lavatera rosea*, with cool pink, single flowers shaped like little hollyhocks. This is perhaps the longest-flowering plant in the whole garden; for at least four months the display goes on, and it grows into a large shrub, despite the fact that it is cut back hard in spring. It enjoys drought and survives wind; it even seeds itself, so that if I lose one in a sharp frost I can find a replacement. I like to have two, one at each end of the border, and its flowers are so cool and blue a pink that I allow my faithful clumps of *Achillea* 'Gold Plate' to mingle with them; the warm gold plates prevent the pink mallow flowers from looking sickly.

My most faithful pink is a penstemon I bought ten years ago before I realised that I needed at least three-of-a-kind of everything. But it has spread and layered itself and altogether fills an important space, half-way down the border in the front. Like the mallow, it flowers for about four months. Its spikes of lovely drooping bells, reminiscent of a foxglove's but more delicate and slightly frilled, contrast with all the other herbaceous shapes – the spikes and plates and daisy flowers. It is a sort of cherry, or rosy garnet, giving a transfusion of life to the surrounding pastels. Penstemons are treasures (I have recently planted a mauvish-blue one, also very pretty but less life-giving), and if some are of indifferent hardiness, others clearly are of sterling constitution; they even keep their leaves in a mild winter, behaving like little woody shrubs; I cut them back along with all the other woody things in spring, and they respond with fresh, less wizened stems.

Other useful pinks in the border are: *Lythrum virgatum*, 'the Rocket', surviving dry summers with reasonable fortitude but never yet quite giving the show it does when growing wild beside a stream in its native form of purple loosestrife; *Echinacea purpurea* 'Robert Bloom', an August flowering daisy with a frill of drooping pink petals round a domed red-brown centre (hence its pet name of 'cone flower'), beautifully upright in its two foot growth (it used to be classified as a rudbekia, but its name has changed in the mysterious way that botanists understand);

Anemone japonica 'September Charm', which in fact begins to flower in August and, now that it is established, pays ever-increasing dividends, quietly spreading and growing taller each year, so that I have enough of it now to move bits of it about the garden, an exercise it does not enjoy; it sulks for about three years before adopting, and adorning, its new place. It is a paradoxical plant, immensely strong in its stems and impervious to rain, shade, wind, drought, and yet so delicate in the detail of its innocent round five-petalled flowers, each flower standing quite alone on its graceful stem with a little green eye fringed with yellow stamens, and a myriad of little rounded buds standing equally alone on their stems, waiting to flower, not to mention the pretty round dead heads still standing erect on theirs, that the whole thing is worthy to be painted on porcelain or printed on chintz.

Of similar colour, pale cool pink with just a hint of mauve, is *Sidalcea* 'Loveliness' – but not of similar constitution. Sidalcea stems have a trick of falling clean over at ground level if you brush by them roughly, reaching for a weed in the border, and they do not like drought. It is a pity they do not make a better show, for when they are on form they are exceptionally pretty: each of their flowers is like a tiny round mallow flower, all arranged together up a stem with the bottom flowers opening first and the top still budded, giving that tapered effect which is the charm of spired flowers – like a hollyhock for a fairy's garden, except that each plant has many stems.

Near indestructible, in contrast, is *Polygonum campanulatum*, blooming for at least three months with dainty bells of white and pink, and spreading grey-green leaves. One plant will fill a two foot square.

Finally, amongst my pink flowers is *Sedum spectabile* 'Autumn Joy', a superb, architectural plant, taking shapes of balanced symmetry throughout the year. It furnishes the front corner of a border to perfection, because it is both bold and short, both solid-looking and adaptable; its spreading, succu-

lent, blue-green leaves are a foil for its flat flower-heads —
flower-heads that run through as many colour mutations as a
hydrangea; in early summer they are green; in August, pink; in
September they turn deep rose; in October, russet. All winter
long they seem to last, in their tawny colours, as dried flowers;
they are the only winter flower-heads to decorate the dead
border. They divide most willingly — indeed, they need to be
divided or they would grow too tall. At about one foot or
fourteen inches, they are supreme.

There is a group of flowers in my border whose colour stands
between pink and white, a washed-out pink or greyish-white,
often mixed with green; the sidalcea only just escapes being
grouped here, for its pink is shell-pale. But paler still are some of
the beauties of the border: *Campanula lactifolia* 'Loddon
Anna', a winner with huge heads of pink-white flowers, each
floweret an upstanding bell; it is at least three feet high and
blooms from June to late July; as the catalogues might claim:
indispensible. Another tall plant of washed-out colour mixing
white and pink with green is the grand herbaceous *Valerian
sambucifolia*: August flowering, self-seeding, at least four feet
high, and the only plant I have yet found with sculptured flat
heads to balance *Achillea* 'Gold Plate'. It romps about its
allotted section of the border and flops sideways in a wind, but is
sufficiently coarse for this not to seem to matter. Also tall,
spreading, and to that extent coarse, is *Macleaya cordata* —
though its creamy buff flower-heads are too delicate to warrant
this unkind word; they are starry plumes (its pet name is the
plume poppy). As it ages, it acquires a hint of bronze; its leaves
are rounded, cabbage green, sycamore-shaped; so far, after four
years, it is only five feet tall and has not spread beyond its
allotted space, and coming into its own half-way through
August it is welcome. It, and the blue echinops, are the two
tallest plants in my border. Finally, also coarse, also mildly
spreading, is *Acanthus longifolius*: once planted never to be
eradicated. I have tried to dig it up and move it elsewhere, but

this only means that it is growing in two places where before it grew in one. And yet I do not want to eradicate it; its long, stiff flower-heads are abundant, and look more prickly than they are; they are hooded in mole-colour, white-veined with green underneath, a sombre and subtle mixture, standing for weeks and weeks but at their best in August; the Greeks knew that their leaves are handsome, and used them in the capitals of Corinthian columns; for this reason, the plants should grow where their arching leaves are not hidden by other flowers; they are sculptured plants; mine mark the end of the border, near the front.

In addition to the pink/white/green group, I have now the beginnings of a group of sharp yellow-green. Here belong not only the splendid columnar flower-heads of *Euphorbia wulfenii* at the far end of the border, and not only the flat heads of *Sedum spectabile* 'Autumn Joy' at the near end, but the sharp and lovely *Alchemilla mollis*, acid green in its flowers, blue-green in its dew-drop-holding, shell-shaped leaves, rounded and well-furnished in its shape; it is one of the most harmonious plants in anybody's garden, pretty for seven months on end, a link plant whose quiet presence enhances the beauty of other plants, and even stops clashing beauties from quarrelling with each other, either in a border or in a vase; and it is not only gentle, but generous – self-seeding itself so prodigally, once established, that it becomes necessary to throw many of its progeny away. The pain of demolishing its pretty seedlings is the only pain it causes – but one can't have every border in the garden edged with *Alchemilla mollis*.

Of pure white flowers I have, so far, only four examples: a white cone flower, *Echinacea purpurea* 'White Lustre', growing behind the pink one, white yellow cone-shaped centres beloved of peacock butterflies; *Physostegia virginica* 'Summer Snow', well named the 'obedient plant', for it does just what it is required to do, grows neatly in the front of the border, only ten inches tall, and throws up long-lasting spikes of dazzlingly white flowers, more striking and reliably floriferous than the pink physostegias I tried at first. Then there is a soaring white *Veronica virginica* 'Alba', a three star plant, with elegant and tender spires, three feet high, that lasts for weeks; and soaring higher still, the graceful bugsbane, *Cimicifuga racemosa*, whose soft ivory racemes of tiny flowers seem so light that they can reach to five feet without any need of a stake. Finally, there is a plant which is such a glistening white that it is almost silver: *Anaphalis yedoensis*, with flat clustered heads of rather dry little flowers which prove, in fact, to be virtually everlasting. It is a spreader, with silver leaves, and I like it best when it does not grow too tall – height does not suit it. I have read that if you keep moving it about, you stunt it, and this I mean to do; it is an excellent foil for other things.

What other things? That is the eternal question with the herbaceous border; it is never finished and never could be finished. A list of the things that have disappeared or had to be scrapped – above all my much-loved border phlox, eel-worm-infested – would make a sorry tale; things fade out; new things come; clumps must be divided, groupings must be improved. On summer evenings, I sit and look along the border and ask myself what it most needs to make it better. Sometimes it is too tall at one end; some tall things must be moved to the other end for balance; sometimes it needs more low-growing things in front (and of course, being an island, it has two fronts); some-times, although the front is low, it is all too similar; *Sedum spectabile, Geranium grandiflora, Alchemilla mollis* – an easy alternation of monotonously rounded humps. Spikes and spires are needed to break them up.

I have at last persuaded a red hot poker seedling to survive the winter and multiply by easy division in the spring. As it gives offence to many people in its brazen orange tipped with gold, I have moved it to the very farthest end of the border where it has the dull glaucous green of *Euphorbia wulfenii* as foil. The spires of white veronica are good against the round blue globe thistle and the flat *Achillea* 'Gold Plate'; the round pink flowers of the Japanese anemones wave above the clustered mass of golden rod; it is pretty to see the pink and white daisies of the echinaceas through perovskia's branching blue spikes, or to see the blue thimbles of the sea holly, eryngium, against the taller yellow daisies of heliopsis and the feathery cream spires of the plume poppy, *Macleaya cordata*. Again, the perovskia's spikes look good mixed with the creamy spikes of *Artemesia lactiflora* – the colours are different, the shapes the same. For contrast is needed and harmony is needed; these are the two opposing poles between which the design of the border is suspended.

At present, what my border needs is brown; tawny warmth, amongst all those lemons, mauves and pinks and blues; crimson is fatal to it, scarlet would upset it, but browns would make it glow. My gaillardias, with their rich mahogany centres, have died out, as gaillardias are inclined to do; I have only one feeble plant left of the brown helenium, 'Moerheim Beauty', but it is enough to tell me I need more. I can do what Vita Sackville-West recommended to all garden planners and planters; pick a stem of it and stick it into the border somewhere else, then stand back and see if that is the place where it should go.

A herbaceous border will always look its best viewed, not broadside on, but from one end; ideally, it should therefore run at right angles to the house windows, or to the garden seat. Fortunately, this is what ours does; from our sitting room window, or from the seat beneath it, there is a long, oblique view down the border. And so, as I sit and survey it in the flattering evening light of summer, it gives me food for dreams; in my imagination, I adjust the counters that the game is played with; the contrasts and the harmonies, the colours and the shapes, the heights and the depths, in the quest of the impossible dream: perfection.

VI

The Hedges

In the second autumn of our garden, we planted hedges. Thus we gave ourselves eighteen months in which to wonder where to put them. It was the hardest and most crucial question that we faced. For with hedges we intended to give our garden shape.

It is difficult to invent a garden. Most of us are influenced by gardens we have seen. We liked the sort of garden that is subdivided into 'rooms', the garden that leads you on from one section to another, where you never know what you will find beyond the arch, down the steps, round the next corner; gardens within gardens. We were influenced by the two great twentieth-century gardens, Hidcote and Sissinghurst. But it was difficult to see how we could apply the lessons of those great gardens here. With formal hedges, yes; but where were the hedges to go? I scribbled on bits of paper; I concocted grandiose schemes; a vast semi-circular sweep, to the south of the herbaceous border, broken in the middle to give a cunning vista of the meadow; at its most ambitious, this sweep was to be a hedge on stilts; pleached limes. I suspected, even as I drew it, that it was not to be. It would be foolish to place a hedge where it would block out half our future view. What we wanted our hedges to do, immediately, was to relate the herbaceous border to the house.

For there the border lay, amongst the tousled space, all on its own, ten yards away from the house and not in line with it. We could not run a hedge the whole length of it, lovely as a hedge may be as a background to herbaceous flowers, because if the hedge was on its southern side it would block both sun and view, and if it were on its northern side we would no longer be able to see the border from the house. Besides, a hedge along the border would contravene the whole sound horticultural principle of the island bed.

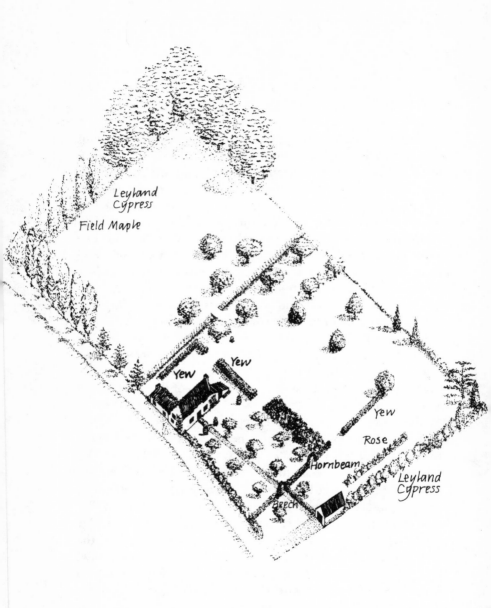

We plant our first hedges.

We could, however, run a hedge across the far end of the border, at right angles to its main axis, without destroying the airy growing conditions of its plants. It might then look as though the hedge had been there first, and the border had grown out from it, was attached to it. Garden beds have this need – to be attached to something. So there was one hedge decided – we would run a hedge across the far end of the border and continue it across the grass to reach the gravel path. But this still did not solve the problem of relating the herbaceous border to the house.

In the end, our plan was simple: we planted a hedge to continue the line of the herbaceous border along below the southern end of the house. It was as though a giant ruler had been put down on the ground: nineteen yards ruled for the herbaceous border, then a short gap, and then fifteen yards ruled for a hedge on the same plane. To complete the idea, we made this hedge turn a right-angle corner when it had passed the house and run northwards back to the lane, forming an 'L' shape, a complementary 'L' to the 'L' of the house. In this way, we contrived an enclosed, courtyard garden, a square of which two sides were supplied by the L-shaped cottage, and two by the L-shaped hedge. And we gained shelter from the east wind. The plan has worked: as you walk along the hedge below the cottage your eye travels straight onwards along the border. As you walk back along the border towards the house, your eye runs along the dark enclosing wall of hedge. As you look out from the kitchen window, there is a cottage wall to your right, a wall of hedge to your left, and straight ahead a wide gap, a view through the hedge to the Italian vase, the cherry trees, and whatever else lies beyond. This gap in the hedge was an essential feature of the plan; to surround the cottage with unbroken hedge would have been unthinkable, but a hedge with a gap in it serves to focus and define a view. (See Plate 3a.) On either side of this gap the hedge is allowed to grow a little higher than the rest and clipped to form a fat, square bastion. These squat castellations are the nearest thing to topiary that we have yet attempted. Whatever mistakes we have made in this garden, this hedge is a success; it ties things together and gives stability and peace. The cottage is now cradled in clipped yew.

For we had no trouble in choosing our hedging plants – the only trouble was in paying for them. Yew was our first choice, right for the old cottage, right for our English theme. And we both loved yew, anyway. We would have had it everywhere, had it not been so expensive.

There is a particular exhilaration and fulfilment in planting a yew hedge. First of all, the little plants themselves are marvellously sturdy. Originally, we ordered seventy-five, each about eighteen inches tall and, to save money, I collected them myself from a north Norfolk nursery in a Ford Cortina estate car. They filled it, floor to ceiling, dashboard to rear gate, piled thickly together and smelling earthily alive, and I drove back across the county on quiet side roads with only a peep-hole out of the windscreen ahead, cradled, as our cottage was to be, in yew. As soon as we got those plants into the ground, they looked settled. Yew is always settled, from the start; it does not, for example, blow or rustle in the wind. It sits there firmly in the ground, and it shows up. How can people complain that it is slow-growing? When it was only eighteen inches high, on the day we had planted it, it transformed the scene. Yew rules its dark, fat line across the ground wherever you want it to go. It is instant hedging. Each year it grows better. To watch it grow, in the spring, is a pleasure. Its young shoots take on different tints; pale green, buff, beige and apricot, these growths are soft and droop a little downwards. By August, they have darkened, stiffened; they are ready to be clipped. My husband clipped the sides of the yew hedges annually in August from the start, but he left the tops untouched until they reached the required height; this, on our eastern flank, was to be eight feet, and it reached it in ten years. The rate at which yew grows varies with the rainfall; in a wet year, it can grow a foot; in a dry year, it barely grows at all. But it is a moment worth waiting for when you can straighten the top of the yew hedge and achieve a neatness so precise and tailored that it will make up for all manner of neglected untidiness and ill-thought-out planting in the beds below.

For a yew hedge makes the perfect background to flowers. This is partly because of its velvet darkness, and partly because of its texture, close-piled as a carpet. It is also a perfect background to plain lawn. There is no simpler but more satisfying garden scene than a stretch of turf sweeping to meet a line of yew hedge; we saw this somewhere and determined to copy it; a few years after our original hedge planting, we extended the hedge that runs across the border's end right across the grass to the bottom of the garden, and we used yew. The top of this hedge is tiered in three descending steps, following the gentle fall of the ground. For some reason this makes it look inevitable; if it had been the same height from end to end it would have looked arbitrary and clumsy. Grass-green meets yew-green – a very simple modulation on the theme of green, where one tone seems to have caught sunshine within it, and the other – shadow.

There is another variation on this theme of green: it is the slight shift of darkness between yew and box, that second evergreen hedging plant of old-fashioned gardens. If yew leans towards blue, box leans towards yellow. It might sound as though they would do nothing for each other side by side; in fact they make a complementary pair. It is partly a matter of texture: the small round leaves of box have a sheen; yew is velvet-dull. They are like contrasting weaves in a single piece of damasked cloth.

At first we bought a bit of dwarf box edging, *Buxus* 'Suffruticosa', in a local market where a nurseryman was selling off his stock. We put it in a semi-circle round the base of the Italian vase which stands between bastions of yew. We have never seen it on sale since; it fell from favour years ago along with labour-

intensive gardening, and was disparagingly described as a har-
bourer of slugs. I think it is about to make a minor comeback.
Meanwhile, we have found a local source of inexpensive *Buxus
sempervirens*, the common box, and bought some to make low
hedges beside the garden doorstep and for a yard or two along
the gravel path towards the Irish yews. It shares with yew an
immediate impression of maturity and permanence, so that
recently a visitor, pointing to our young box hedges, delighted
us by saying:

'Were those there when you bought the cottage?'

'No,' we said smugly.

Box is *really* slow growing, much slower than yew. There
seems no foreseeable danger of our little hedges growing beyond
two feet tall. It clips beautifully, just as beautifully as yew and,
like yew, it only needs clipping once a year. So pleased with
the sturdy box plants have we become that we have used a
few single specimens as markers, redeeming otherwise feeble
corners of flower borders with that simplest shape in topiary – a
ball of box.

The first hedge we planted, the one that runs from path to end
of border, is made of hornbeam. Hornbeam grows with exciting
speed, is easy to establish, clips beautifully, and is altogether an
excellent hedging plant. People mistake it for beech. But it is not
quite as beautiful as beech. There is a shine on a beech leaf and a
beauty of fresh green which is a little muted on the hornbeam;
hornbeam leaves have a suggestion of crinkled pleats, they are
so crisply ruled with veins. They hold their leaves in winter, too,
but not quite as long as beech does, and they are yellow in
autumn, very nice, but lacking the beech's russet glories. In
winter, they take on the colour of milky coffee while the beech
is cinnamon brown. However, beech is difficult to establish;
indeed, the first year after you plant a beech hedge, the little trees
look really weedy. They do not seem able to grow at all; some of
them even go backwards, dying at the tips; some of them do
actually die. We filled gaps in the hedge along the lane with

beech and lost almost half our trees. Because we love beech, we tried again, filling the sad spaces with new plants until, at last, they 'took' and made a hedge. One gap we filled with copper beech, mixed with hornbeam and holly (the holly grew from a berry on a Christmas front door wreath): a 'tapestry hedge' with the shining bottle green of holly, the shining port wine of coppery beech, is an exhilarating sight. A few years later, when the time came to make a kitchen garden in our field, we hedged most of it with clipped beech too. (Weakly, and wrongly, we planted quick growing privet down the further side, in too much hurry to gain privacy from our neighbours. Now the privet needs trimming three times a year, has extra-greedy roots, and looks plain dull.)

We would not be without our neat and lovely hedges – hornbeam, beech, changing with the seasons. They cannot make quite so beautiful a hedge as yew, but they enhance the autumn garden quite spectacularly with russet and gold, and their comforting brown leaves are the beauty of our winter.

We seldom prepared the trenches that were to receive our hedging plants with the care they deserved; we always seemed to be in a desperate rush. When possible, we manured them first; occasionally we mulched them afterwards, but in the early years all our hedges had to struggle with couch grass and lesser weeds, and I had to struggle along those ever-lengthening stretches of hedge, weeding. Those days are gone; little will grow now under the thick yew hedges – even the rain seldom penetrates there; and the beech and hornbeam, fully grown, mulch their own beds each spring with their own crunchy, fallen leaves – the best leaf-mould there is.

The hedge we inherited along the lane is a mixed country hedge of hawthorn, lilac, sloe, elder, snowberry and elm. The snowberry is a feeble plant and cannot grow as tall as its neighbours. This is unfortunate, because after a year or two, when the highway on the horizon was still troubling us, we hit upon the plan of letting these boundary hedges along the lane grow really tall; it was the best way of cutting out our skyline while waiting for our trees to grow. These rough old hedges obligingly grew to twelve feet and more; we trimmed them as far as we could reach and let them blouse out above, like many half-trimmed old hedges canopying English country lanes. But now Dutch elm disease is here, and most of the elms have died. Perhaps we shall replace them with the excellent thick, speedy hornbeam; perhaps we shall try to extend the excitement of our strip of tapestry, and fill in with coppery beech; we probably won't use hawthorn – it's too prickly at pruning time; we may stick to the rough country hedge idea, in which case we may fill the gaps with field maple, *Acer campestre*. We have already used this, with great success, down a side boundary ditch.

For we had our long side boundaries to consider; on either flank we were exposed to our neighbours' view. So when our subdividing hedges, our yew and hornbeam, were safely in, and our main tree planting done, an autumn came when we could afford to consider our flanks. Here, far from the house and flower garden, near the shaggy ditches that marked our boundaries, neat formal hedging would be inappropriate. That is why we chose field maple for one long stretch. This maple is a splendid hedging plant: robust, quite fast growing, with small, fine-cut maple leaves that are pink in spring, green in summer and in autumn turn a brilliant gold; it puts up with weeds and drought, and will easily grow ten feet high. A long strip of it is lovely, but it will also look at home in a mixed country hedge.

It is a pity we did not have the courage of our convictions: we should have planted maple from end to end of our eastern boundary. But we did not trust it; the books said it was fast growing, and we did not trust them either; we decided to plant the most vulnerable stretch of our eastern boundary, where we looked straight onto the old poultry farm house, with that standby of those who panic in their desire for instant privacy: Leyland cypresses.

Everyone knows it: × *Cupressocyparis leylandii*, the wonder, and now the scapegoat and scourge, of the gardening world. It grows so fast that you can almost watch it growing; the younger it is the faster it grows, putting on perhaps three feet in a year; after seven years it will slow down. One wonders how long-lived it will be. Will it not wear itself out to an early death with all this energetic growing? At any rate, we panicked to the east and we panicked to the west; we put rows of Leyland cypresses along the most exposed stretches of both our boundaries, a double row on the west. It is churlish to be sniffy about this tree, when it is no trouble and does its job so well. There it stands now, the back rank on our western edge, sixteen feet tall, a pleasant cypress green, thick but unobtrusive, with soft cypressy plumes on branches growing neatly upwards towards the sky. It has made an important difference to our windswept garden. Indeed, thanks to its towering presence, our garden is no longer windy. Sometimes, when winds buffet the surrounding fields, a tall wand of Leyland is snapped, and dangles pitifully in the wake of the storm. Below it, the garden is unscathed. But – it is not right here. It does not speak the same language as the old cottage; it has nothing to say to the willows and the hawthorn and the ash; it is a forward, modern upstart, a superbly efficient example of hybridising skill; whoever Leyland was, his name is rightly immortalised in the tree with which, all over England, people are blocking out unwanted views of other people.

To minimise their wrongness of shape and spirit, we treat the front ranks of our Leyland cypresses as hedge. They put up meekly with clipping, indeed they look better clipped; in August one of us mounts a ladder and, with one of those long-handled pruners that operate with a lever and wire, attempts to hook the waving topmost Leyland plumes and cut them off. They tumble down upon our heads, soft two foot sprays of cypress, and they exude some strangely drying exhalation so that, after half-an-hour of work amongst them, we must rush for cups of tea. Then we come back and go on stretching, hooking for wayward plumes we have missed, until at last we have achieved an appearance of flat-topped hedge, twelve feet high; and then they cease to jar upon the eye, for it is their spindly, pointed growing tips that fit so badly with this landscape. So there they stand, a formidable screen, swallowing up sounds as well as sights and gales.

In front of the Leylands on our western boundary we have an informal, arching hedge of roses. In fact, the roses were there first. It was only when they proved inadequate as a screen that we introduced the Leyland row behind them. Now the Leylands make a becoming background to the roses and, as if inspired by those tall trees, or perhaps entering into a competition for light and air, the roses themselves are growing taller and taller, throwing giant wands up towards the sky. They are the *xanthina* hybrid shrub rose 'Canary Bird'. When this rose hedge flowers, it is a light-hearted thing: the canary-coloured flowers are single, and prettily carried all along the arching branches in May and June, and the leaves are soft and fernlike, dull green like the Leyland's foliage. They go well together. Often a bright green coarse-leaved sucker shoots up six feet amongst the ferny leaves and I have to crawl through the dark, dry caverns between the towering Leylands and the towering roses, searching the source of the sucker with my trowel. We do not use shears when trimming this rose hedge, but only restrain its untidiness with a snip of the secateurs here and there, so that it is not so much a hedge as a bank of roses.

A flowering hedge obviously serves a different purpose from a trimmed and formal one; it does not give structure or outline a plan; it is an ornament, not the bones of a garden, but its flesh. I would not want to use an ornamental flowering hedge to mark the divisions within a garden – it would be too forward, too distracting, calling attention to itself; it is less like a wall than a wall-paper. The satisfaction of a well-trimmed formal hedge lies in the quiet uniformity of its colour and the close texture of its leaves; they learn to lie thick and flat, overlapping each other, and present an almost continuous surface to the eye and hand.

There remains a fascination in flowering hedges. We have four lilacs in front of the Leylands further down the boundary, beyond 'Canarybird'. These, too, were planted first, intended as a screen of free-growing shrubs against next door; now the Leylands grow behind them and they are rather squashed; one day, perhaps, we will clip the lilac, and they will become as one with the cypress hedge, it will carry them on its surface as a flowering camouflage. They are old-fashioned lilacs, strong growing and strong scented, their blooms mostly double, like clotted cream; 'Souvenir de Louis Späth', plum coloured; 'Katherine Havemeyer', lavender; 'Firmament', a lovely pale double, washy pink opening to washy blue. Perhaps we won't see so much of them when they are clipped; just a lovely fat clustered flower-head hiding here and there under its leaves as lilac flowers do.

We tried another lilac hedge, guided fatally by book or catalogue. And this was intended as a dividing hedge, near the garden shed. We had never seen these persian lilacs, *Syringa* × *persica*, but we liked the sound of them, and read that they would make a pretty, lacy hedge. They proved impossibly flimsy, small leafed, thin twigged; the air showed through them. They were struggling in an unsympathetic bit of ground. True, their single flowers were delightful, starry, lilac-coloured; but in the end we moved them, to try a new life, not as hedging plants, but as widely-spaced, single specimens along the garden path. And a row of our tested favourite, beech, is making a proper dividing hedge where the lilacs were.

So now we are hedged in. We have privacy, the first need of a garden; and we are beginning to have a little of that sense of mystery which is a garden's second need. No longer can we see the whole thing at once. That was what was wrong with our place at first; its whole despondent blankness was immediately apparent. We can walk down the border and through an arch in the hornbeam hedge into a 'secret garden', invisible from the house; we can return through a gap between hornbeam and yew and find ourselves upon the lower lawn. We can stand outside our kitchen door in a courtyard enclosed in yew.

The price of these hedges is paid in my husband's chronically aching shoulders. He has calculated that there is a total of 340 yards to cut each summer. Originally he trimmed them all with a favoured pair of Wilkinson shears, standing on heavy old wooden steps to do the tops. Now we have light aluminium steps and an electric hedge cutter, with yards of electric cable trailing. It is quite heavy to hold and can never supply the beautifully exact finish of hand shears; always there are a few bruised and bungled cuts. But it is quick.

At least we have now cut one hedge right down; the old, overgrown hedge at the bottom of the garden, that hid our view of the water meadows beyond.

VII

The Herbs and the Annuals

In my original imaginings, I had seen the space inside the 'L' of the house as a paved garden. But as soon as we moved in I saw it as a herb garden, partly because it would cost too much to pave it all, and partly because it was just outside the kitchen door. It would be nice to rush out, in the middle of dishing up a meal, and pick a sprig of something as a garnish; besides, herbs would surely smell good, near the house. A herb garden means, to me, a pattern of beds and paving; a herb garden would not look right with grass all round it, and if it did not consist of several beds, but only of one, then it would not be a herb garden at all, but simply a herb bed. It should aspire towards neatness and symmetry of lay-out; herbs, not especially tidy things, can be arranged tidily; the simplest way to tidy them is to put a neat dwarf hedge round each bed, and paving beyond that. With these ideas, we started.

A builder produced a pile of 'pamments', the old, rosy flooring tiles of Norfolk cottages; the first autumn we had one modest square of paving laid; it looked as if it had always been there; as soon as we could find more 'pamments', we laid another. They were then like two of the paler squares on a chess board, corner to corner, and between them, corner to corner, the dark squares were provided by the two herb beds. This layout has been modified and the beds extended round three sides of the paving in later years, but the initial idea of squareness and symmetry persists. And so do the neat, trimmed hedges.

The hedges did not have to be the same all round; one side could be one thing, one side another, and where they met, a taller, aromatic shrub could pinpoint the corner. I could have the dwarf Hidcote lavender on one face, cotton lavender on the

Our paved herb and peach gardens.

other; for punctuation marks at the corners I could have two bushes of rosemary here, two bushes of southernwood there.

'Hidcote' lavender, Daniel's variety is, when it is still in bud, the deepest purple velvet lavender there is. Each winter it looks starved and ramshackle, bits of it tend to break off at the root and I wonder, as I half-heartedly dig out bits of creeping buttercup from its base, whether the summer transformation can ever happen again, making it almost overnight a rounded, healthy, leafy plant crowned with dense stems of scented purple. So far it has always happened. I have never had to renew my plants, and the only attention they get, apart from cursory weeding, is the sad chopping down of their dried and faded flower stems in September. It is sad because one can persuade oneself that the flower heads still look nice, even in death. I leave them as long as I can; for two months they adorn the garden, though the deep purple fades as the buds open into flowers.

My cotton lavender, *Santolina chamaecyparissus* 'Nana' is supposedly dwarf too, as its name implies, though it does its best each year to grow beyond its 'nana' name. I bought little plants of it at a garden stall in my second summer, and have had it, or its replacements, ever since. I keep it in bounds by trimming it not once but twice a year: in April, when it is just starting into growth, and again in August, slicing its aromatic silver cotton with shears to get a straight top and straight edges. It takes a strong nerve to do this, for the soft little growths dress the plant becomingly and it looks naked after the shearing, like sheep whose shining fleeces lie upon the floor; but it has to be done, otherwise the plants would straggle, spread and die. The reward comes quickly: a lovely fat neat edging hedge of solid silver, silver as the alba willow, a foot high and a foot thick. It is not allowed to flower, either; as soon as it starts to produce the little silver buds which will turn into little yellow globes, I shear them off for they, too, are a threat to the solidity of the hedge; allow them to flower, and they will grow tall, and make a gap in the hedge where they were. I cannot imagine this garden without its cotton lavender hedges now; for all their softness, they have become part of its bone structure. In hard winters some plants die; I used to buy new ones; now I am learning to build up a supply from cuttings.

The corner rosemary bushes also come and go. A hard winter will always threaten them. Just as a rosemary had grown into the really dominant plant it is required to be in the symmetrical lay-out, taller than the santolina, taller than the lavender, a hard frost will strike it and it will die. Then a new little rosemary plant will take over, though lately I have learnt a simple anti-frost technique: a plastic carrier bag, slit at the bottom and then slipped over the plant and held with four stout stakes pushed down into the earth inside it at each corner, turning the bag into a taut plastic square. The rosemary lives on inside its plastic walls, protected from winds but open to the light of the sky. The variety I grow is supposedly upright, 'Miss Jessop', but mine never retains that neat, cypress-like habit, and in no time at all it is leaning its elbows on the paving, sprawling about and getting in the way. Yet its ascending growing tips are very beautiful; I give it its head; I do not prune it, except when picking sprigs to flavour pork and lamb and courgettes; I love its untidiness, and the hint of silver under the sharp little dark green leaves, its potent resinous scent, and its smoke-blue flowers in spring.

In a complementary corner to the rosemary's grows the curry plant, *Helichrysum angustifolium*. The peculiar value of this little silver shrub is that its curry scent hangs on the air in winter and very early spring. If a herb garden is to look and smell good in winter, the curry plant with its tiny yellow everlasting flowers is the thing to go for.

The artemesias, marking two other corners, are more reliable than the rosemaries and even more beloved; they are *Artemisia abrotanum*, the old-fashioned herb with the wide choice of pet names: old man, lad's love or – simply – southernwood. Old man suggests, perhaps, their bedraggled appearance in winter, when they look half-dead and whiskery, for they are not evergreen. Lad's love suggests their fresh green vigorous growth in

May; and perhaps southernwood carries a hint of their warm, fresh, delicious scent. They are planted close together, opposite each other, where two corners of the chess board meet, and they brush against you as you walk between them. I never pass in summer without pinching a bit of southernwood and crushing it in my fingers; it has a sharp apple scent. Sprigs of southernwood laid in drawers are supposed to discourage moths. Each spring, I chop them right down hard to the base of last year's growth; each summer they have become again great fat bushes with countless ascending stems of gentle, feathery green.

These plants, the lavender and cotton lavender, the rosemary and southernwood, were the frames of my herb garden. But what should grow inside them? I could not fill the entire beds with the herbs I use for cooking. I would need decorative things as well. One has only to look at a herb grower's catalogue to see that 'herbs' go beyond the culinary: there are medicinal herbs too, and if you count all the plants the old herbalists used, you approach a list unnervingly reminiscent of a herbaceous border. It could include monkshood and bergamot, salvia and hyssop, foxgloves and mullein, valerian and sea holly, catmint and evening primrose, globe thistle and *Alchemilla mollis*; it could include sweet briar roses. So I could grow whatever aromatic plants I liked, mix them with the herbs we like for flavour, and call it a herb garden; a herb garden need not exist exclusively in shades of grey and green.

However, the culinary herbs come first: tarragon, the French variety, not the Russian which is tasteless, though it looks the same; parsley, needing to be sown each year unless it has run to seed and sown itself; I pour boiling water from a kettle along the seed drill before sowing it, to warm up the soil and speed it on; apple mint, a well-flavoured, tall, furry mint which needs to be trapped in a corner by itself to stop it spreading; it grows right beside our kitchen door-step, and in July it flowers with tiny white flower-heads that grow up towards the pink-flowered jasmine round the porch. It is both juicy and furry at the same time. Then there is the purple-leaved sage, much prettier than the green one; lemon thyme, needing a sunny spot in which to spread out with its pretty pink and white flowers; the ornamental golden marjoram, *Origanum vulgare* 'Aureum', also an easy spreader in the sun with delightful leaves and pretty flower-heads like the thyme's, but delicious in cooking or as a garnish, too; chives, so amenable that it will put up with long life in a shallow pottery trough, provided it is in the sun; sorrel, like a well-behaved and perennial spinach, always producing new leaves for soup, however greedily it is picked; winter savory, available all the year round, in summer, too, despite its name; finally, the most delicious of all herbs, the peppery sweet basil, which unfortunately is half-hardy and an annual; I buy small potted plants at the end of May and bed them in a sunny place.

Of slightly taller herbs, medicinal and decorative, I have borage, for the sake of its blue flowers; it is an annual, and I only sowed it once, but its descendants are still with me, for it is a prolific self-seeder; then I have lemon balm, *Melissa officianalis* 'Aurea', for the sake of its golden variegated leaves. If you are not careful it will seed itself everywhere and its progeny are plain green, so it is wise to chop off all its flower-heads at midsummer and generally keep it within bounds, for it is a perennial and will be there again, a brilliant gold, next spring.

I have some towering herbs which can be used for cooking, too. There is angelica, a statuesque biennial with large, bright green, sharp-cut leaves, extremely decorative, sending up a central stalk like a hollow trunk crowned with domed flower-heads, six feet high, like giant hemlock; in theory the bright green jointed stalks can be crystallised and used on top of a child's birthday cake. It seeds itself vigorously once established, and one needs to be strong-minded about digging up the surplus flourishing, healthy young plants. They make good presents for the growing band of angelica-fanciers. It is even harder to chop the noble parent plant down. Its umbels turn to spectacular starry seedheads where acrobatic blue tits swing and feed and, as the leaves die, the stems turn pink. It is difficult to decide when death, in the angelica, has ceased to be beautiful. At the other end of the scale is comfrey, an untidy invader which exists only to be chopped down, for its leaves, once valued for their healing properties, are now valued by organic gardeners as a rich source of protein if the wilted leaves are spread at the bottom of a trench in which, for example, potatoes are to be planted. It is like a very unshowy anchusa, with washed-out blue flowers, and I keep it strictly in its place, cutting it down at least twice each summer.

Fennel is another tall perennial herb which seeds itself freely: I find those tell-tale, misty little tufts coming up between the cracks in the paving, under concrete steps, everywhere. Nor do I want it everywhere; one plant is quite enough. The importance of my plant to me lies not in its aniseed taste, but in its appearance; its foliage contrasts with all the other foliage in the herb garden. Its leaves are as soft and cloudy as angelica's are well-defined. There is a bronze variety, *Ferula* 'Giant Bronze', which we grow. The bronze diminishes as the season advances and it ends up a dull fennel green, but it first comes through the earth in spring in whorls of soft bronze wool; it grows taller and taller; finally it throws up its filigree flower stems and myriads of flat golden flower-heads, six feet high. It will soften any flower arrangement as surely as it softens any garden with its cloudy beauty; it is at its loveliest after a shower of rain, in spring, when raindrops hang suspended in its mist of fern.

I tried another aniseed-smelling, tallish herb at first: sweet Cicely, a gentle-sounding thing. The plant proved otherwise; apart from the smell of its crushed and lacy leaves, it looked uncannily like cow parsley, and started to occupy too much room; it is not biennial, but perennial, and it is a prodigious self-seeder, not easy to dig up; its strong pink tap root goes down deep into the earth. I got it all up, however, in the end, and replanted it at the very bottom of the garden where it now outdoes the cow parsley and is establishing its colonies.

Lovage is a better proposition: again a perennial, easily raised from seed, with fine-cut leaves and a rare suggestion of celery when chopped, which makes it very useful in the kitchen. For years my lovage grew to five feet tall; recently, however, it has been shooting up to a ridiculous eight feet or so, and each summer I resent the way it blocks my view of other things and cut it down by half.

For the spectacular plant that *makes* my herb garden I turn from the culinary to the ornamental. It was called, when I bought it, clary sage, but I would not think of using its large leaves in stuffing and I suspect it is, in fact, the sage that is also called *Salvia turkestanica*. It belongs to the tribe of biennial self-seeders; I throw away all the spent old plants in autumn and re-arrange the plump and well-developed seedlings in the spots where they should go. I also give away its seedlings to my visitors; it is the most coveted plant in the whole garden. About three feet tall, each stem has a branching candelabrum of flowers, and each plant sends up several stems; the petals are mauve and white; the bracts are pink and green; the effect is opalescent; the plants rise tapering in ranks all round the herb garden; the colour combinations on the wonderful hooked and hooded flowers are ever-changing, like mother-of-pearl tilted in the light; it shimmers all summer long behind the cotton lavender and between the roses. (See Plate 5.)

For I have roses in my herb garden: the apothecary's rose, *Rosa gallica* 'Officinalis', whose parma violet petals retain their scent even when dry, and thus may be harvested for pot pourri; and the discarded floribundas from the herbaceous border – 'Sweet Repose', cream fading with age to strawberry pink. One day a purist fit may seize me and I may move these floribundas. But the fact is that they have settled beautifully amongst the herbs. So have violas and pansies. I treat them as biennials and sow a new packet every year, 'Fancy Shades Mixed', or 'Large Flowered Mixed', moving them to the herb garden where they fill all bare patches with their engaging, many-coloured faces

and flower from springtime onwards until the spreading vegetation of high summer blocks them from the light. I have
strawberries here too, the alpine strawberry 'Baron Solemacher'
raised from seed and now divided regularly to make a pretty and
fruitful edging along the shady side of a bed. There are other
aliens in the herb garden, refugees from other places, things in
transit; the population changes, sometimes I have sweet
williams, sometimes pinks, sometimes hollyhocks, at the back.
Sometimes I think a visitor would not recognise it as a herb
garden at all.

We have another little garden now which is symmetrical and
paved. We devised it after we had been here for about six years,
when herbaceous border and herb garden had taken shape and
our big garden still seemed rather dull and uneventful. As soon
as we had thought of it, it seemed inevitable; all that remained
was to dig it out and lay the paving.

It lies on the south side of the yew hedge, in line with the
herbaceous border. It consists of two square beds, twelve feet
square, with a twelve foot by twelve foot square of paving bricks
laid in herring-bone pattern in between. And it is enclosed on
three sides, for we have extended the yew hedge round it at
either end – it is open only to the south. Thus, when you sit
there, you are sheltered on the north, east and west by yew
hedge, like the back and two arms of a Chesterfield sofa, and
you face the sun. 'That's a nice little spot,' a visitor says, coming
upon it round a corner. But no-one has yet said: 'That's a *pretty*
little spot,' and I am still trying to determine exactly what
plantings suit it best. There is such a temptation, with a new
patch of garden, to fill it with any old thing that comes to hand –
things that clash elsewhere, like some bombastic oriental
poppies, in uncompromising scarlet, which appeared by mistake at the feet of the bright pink 'Zéphirine Drouhin' one
summer and required moving, or like some annual opium
poppies, frilly and salmon, given us by neighbours as seed.

We called it the 'peach garden' because we planted a young

peach tree in the middle of each square bed: 'Peregrine' and 'Rochester', a delicious-sounding pair, lovingly planted in lime-rubble and manure. But every spring, they suffered intolerably from die-back and leaf-curl, despite conscientious, time-taking, money-wasting, miserable spraying. In the end we scrapped them, with a sense of wild relief, before we had a single peach.

So what should be the character of this warm and sheltered garden? Different ideas converged on it.

It should be a winter garden, a sheltered spot where we could enjoy the first tiny bulbs of the year.

It should be a formal garden, with ranks of wallflowers in the spring, bedding plants in summer, and an edging of dwarf box.

It should be a garden of hardy annuals, ephemeral and gay.

It should be a garden with a colour scheme, yellows, golds, reds and orange, to flame against the dark yew hedges.

It *must* be full of bright, sun-loving flowers.

And then we saw that it could be *all* these things.

It starts with winter flowers: two clumps of *Iris unguicularis*; (syn. *I. stylosa*) the delicate, furled buds push up amongst the leaves and you pick them with a sharp pull and watch the slow-motion opening, in a vase, of their large, mauve fleurs-de-lys. They are such a miracle in winter that I endure their clumps of leaves in summer, untidy though they are with a tendency to brown at the tips. Then come other, smaller iris: *Iris reticulata* and *Iris histrioides* 'Major', tiny, sturdy February flowers of astonishing blue in the grey days, and with well-behaved leaves that disappear in summer. With them come colonies of golden winter aconites and washed-out, milky-blue *Scylla tubergeni-ana* – this last a wonderful coloniser and never-fail performer from February onwards, with three or more spikes per bulb, each barely three inches high. With the first hint of spring, a few fat Dutch hybrid crocuses appear along the edges of the beds, for crocuses will only open nicely in a sunny place.

When spring is well under way it is time for an attempt at the formal bedding scheme, with wallflowers tight-packed in a double row round two sides of each bed, a mirror image of each other. I try to select pale wallflowers, for the much-loved mahogany browns would not find a flattering foil in yew. Sutton's 'Persian Carpet' is not bad for my purpose, but the colours I cherish are the creams, pinks and primroses, not the purples and golds. My happiest effect came the year when the little white and yellow annual, *Limnanthes douglasii*, the poached egg flower, bloomed round the base of the wallflowers when they were flowering.

But before the wallflowers have bloomed, their successors must be sown, to take over their space when they are gone. I have tried, and rejected, summer bedding schemes of snapdragons; even when they do well, they smack too much of 'bare-earth gardening', lovely in municipal parks or squares, but wrong in cottage gardens. My aim is to cover the ground so completely with vegetation that the soil cannot be seen at all, so I now favour an exuberant mixture of annuals sown where they are to flower. It is a chancy business, and in a bad year there can be discouraging untidiness and general absence of flowers; it is always haphazard, as the flowers themselves have the final vote on where to flower; but the very spontaneity and lack of conscious planning gives the right antidote to the formal topiary of the setting. So, year after year, the self-seeders reappear: Shirley poppies, shell-pink, coral and white, mix with the baby blue of love-in-a-mist. Amongst these, each year, I make little holes, precisely where I want them, into which I press the big wrinkled seeds of nasturtiums, the pale butter colour 'Peach Melba', splashed with scarlet, and the flame and amber 'Alaska', another dwarf nasturtium but with beautiful cream-marbled leaves. These nasturtiums will always flower profusely and will fill whatever space is available for weeks on end.

Best of all, however, among the annual successors to the wallflowers, are sweet peas: not the climbers, of course, but Thompson and Morgan's spreading carpeter whose sweet-scented and floriferous beauty deserves a better name than 'Snoopea'. I take trouble with this, composting a short trench just behind the wallflowers in late winter and sowing the seed in April, after giving it the regulation softening between damp tissues to wrinkle its horny case. By the time the wallflowers are done, the sweet peas are ready to take over; they have no tendrils and their stems spread horizontally over the available ground, or prop themselves vertically against their neighbours, and soon they are filling all the empty space with flowers, lilac, pink, scarlet and white, clearly superior to all the other hardy annuals, yet in perfect harmony with them.

In practice, however, I have not managed to fill the beds with annuals alone, and have always relied for substance upon other plants as well – pinks, for instance. I have a circle of pinks in the middle of each bed, round the spot where the peaches used to grow: it is made up of the famous salmon-pink 'Doris' interspersed with the dear old white, chocolate-eyed 'Dad's Favourite'. Their rounded clumps of blue-green leaves are pretty even when the flush of flowers is over, and they are superbly floriferous, if floppy; after about three years they have usually flowered themselves out, and must be renewed. I try various methods: sometimes I fill plastic propagating trays, the ones with high, ventilated plastic lids, with John Innes potting compost and stick in the anxiously selected little stems with their touching rosettes of leaves, hoping I've got the conditions right, the moisture right, for rooting; sometimes I try layering, with the help of a kitchen knife and a drum of rooting powder into which I thrust the half-cut stem before attempting to push it down, jaws open, and anchor it in the earth with a large flint – dead easy in the books, more difficult than cuttings in practice, I find, for I tend to get into a tangle, upset the rooting powder, and

5 **In the herb garden:** *Salvia turkestanica*, the spectacular clary sage, dominates the varied greens of lovage and southernwood, its colour combinations ever-changing, like mother-of-pearl tilted in the light.

weeks later absent-mindedly remove the anchoring flint; and sometimes, in a hurry or in despair at the gaps in my circle of pinks, I simply stick likely bits straight into the soil where they are needed and, if it rains, they 'take'. In self-defence at this sketch of amateurism, I must plead that propagating plants is difficult if you are only intermittently there to water them. At any rate, pinks must be *very* easy, for one way and another mine have so far survived.

Behind the pinks, and flowering with them, come one of the undoubted successes of the garden: *Alstroemeria ligtu* hybrids, peach-coloured, apricot and flame, grown from seed, and now appearing everywhere; they even have the insolence to climb through the hedge itself, and the occasional startling coral head bursts from the middle of the sombre wall of yew. They flower for weeks, always look lovely, even when lying sprawled on the ground (for I refuse to stake them) and last magnificently as cut flowers in water.

As summer advances into August and the pinks and alstroemerias rest, I aspire more and more towards the glowing, golden colour-scheme. There are lilies, *L. henryi* in one bed, the grand old tiger lily in the other. *Henryi* is immensely tall and willowy, its great heads of reflexed flowers, barley-sugar coloured with dangling green anthers, look almost too untamed and aristocratic for this place; but tiger lilies are perfect, growing absolutely straight on stout stems, too familiar to be exotic, robust in their orange, dark-spotted glory. Only half as tall as the lilies,

6 a and b Two views of the peach garden: a) Bright flowers growing within a severe frame of yew, dwarf box and low, clipped tables of *Cotoneaster horizontalis*. There is nemesia behind the box edging, and *Alstroemeria ligtu* hybrids circling the central domed and rounded yew. The contours of the yew hedge are echoed in hornbeam at the far end of the herbaceous border.
b) The cottage gable rises above the peach garden. Here you sit at a table on paving between tiger lilies and *Lilium henryi*, a fiery crocosmia insisting on its right to space below.

but blazing beneath them with deeper brilliance, flower some scarlet crocosmias, grand relations of the old monbretia, which look as if they must be difficult and tender, but prove to be easy and hardy. And down at ground level, two clumps of the evening primrose, *Oenothera missouriensis*, spread their succession of sulphur-yellow trumpets over the brick paving.

We have aimed at formality amongst bright disorderliness by planting a line of small box plants as a dwarf hedge across the front of each bed, and two healthy little yew trees, seedlings from the hedges, where the diseased peaches used to grow. They are a stout pair, Gog and Magog, or Tweedledum and Tweedledee, clipped cylindrically, with smaller domes on top, like pawns in a chess set. Two *Cotoneaster horizontalis*, stuck into the front corners of the beds, are ruthlessly clipped too into low, spreading tables, or they would leave scant room for anything else. The severest dark frame to our sheltered garden has thus evolved, all inky yew and box and cotoneaster, but we still call this sunny place the peach garden. (See Plate 6.)

If a strict 'annual garden' proved too difficult a discipline for me to follow, annuals themselves have proved surprisingly easy – or rather, *easy* annuals have proved indispensable, overflowing far beyond the peach garden to fill gaps everywhere. Easy annuals are those you sow where they are to bloom – thus ruling out all the half-hardies that need to be raised in pots and trays under glass, for we have no glass: no greenhouse, no cold frame. If I feel a need for the cheerful brightness of nemesia, I buy half a box of seedlings in May. I always feel a need for the intoxicatingly scented white tobacco plant, *Nicotiana grandiflora*, though often it is almost impossible to run it down amongst the comparatively scentless much-favoured varieties in crimson and lime green.

Buying half-hardy annuals at garden centres is an extravagant answer to the problem. But packets of seeds are cheap. Each year I try to hold back my pen from filling whole columns with crabbed computerised numbers on the seed merchants' order forms. And each year, in midwinter, fat brown envelopes bulging with bright seed packets come through the letter box. Always there are one or two for which I have read rave notices in newspaper articles or books; when they arrive and I read their names I have forgotten what they are. The hardy annual *Nemophila maculata*, for example, turns out to be a sky blue edging plant for moist places, recommended warmly by Robin Lane Fox; *Phacelia campanularia*, not much taller and also blue, turns out to be a good bee plant with scented leaves, much recommended by Vita Sackville-West. I sow most of them, with a mixture of hope and disbelief, and always in a great hurry, in April, when there are a hundred other things to do. I tip the seeds onto a saucer and then sprinkle them with finger and thumb along wobbly drills drawn with a stick in the raked earth. If the weather is dry, I water the drill first; if the seed is a slow germinator, like parsley, I use a kettle of boiling water. I pat the earth back lightly with my hands. Very tiny seeds, like poppies or violas, I shake from their packets broadcast over their allotted patch of earth.

Sometimes the results are thin: mignonette, in particular, seems shy about germinating; I seldom achieve more than three or four plants, but the night-scented stock, *Matthiola bicornis*, is easy. You scarcely notice it by day, a limp and weedy tangle of greyish leaves and stems near the garden door. At dusk the mauve and white flowers open and the mysterious summer scent fills the air. Just the opposite is *Lavatera* 'Mont Blanc', a dazzlingly showy plant by day, two feet high with large chalk-white mallow flowers, yet it, too, germinates in a flower border with ease. My latest recruit to the indispensible annuals list is a member of the borage family, a glorified viper's bugloss: *Echium* 'Blue Bedder', whose seeds are reassuringly big, whose germination is excellent, and whose colour is so concentrated that a patch of it near the front of a border supplies a long-lasting sheet of intense violet blue.

For this is the generosity of annuals: because they only have

one summer in which to reproduce themselves, they flower
prodigiously, particularly if you dead-head them as the first
flowers fade; and if their efforts at reproduction are successful,
their progeny will be flowering away next summer.

It is the same with biennials. Most of these are particularly
good at self-seeding, like the angelica and salvia and borage in
my herb garden. But there are foxgloves too, and sweet rocket,
and scotch thistle, and hollyhocks (I treat these as biennials in
the faltering belief that this discourages the rust to which they
are such martyrs). It is hard to believe that scotch thistles
(*onopordum*) are not perennial; towering up to six or seven feet
with stems like silver trunks, they spread their prickly candel-
abra wide and the gold-finches rejoice; yet they will topple at
one well-aimed stroke of the spade, revealing a ridiculously
small root ball to support all that statuesque growth. Each year,
they must go on the bonfire, leaving countless rosettes of silver
leaves for next year's garden, sometimes brilliantly sited, sometimes quite impertinent. Foxgloves always sow themselves in
prize places and have to be removed. Hollyhocks spring up with
reckless confidence in the midst of low growing plants. Seldom,
however, do the self-seedings come in the choice of colours of
the original selection; the foxgloves seem usually to revert to
ordinary purple, when it is the ravishing apricot or the rare
white 'Alba' that I favour; the self-sown hollyhocks are pre-
dominantly pink. I therefore buy new seed most years, contriving a seed bed somewhere in the garden by midsummer.
Beside the row of foxgloves goes a row of hollyhocks; I love the
double sulphur-yellow, but better still I love the single black –
Althea rosea 'Nigra'. It is in fact a deep claret but as nearly black
as a flower can be, particularly against a white-washed wall.
Beside the row of hollyhock seed goes a row of Canterbury bells,
destined to flower along the gravel path in purple, white and
pink.

By late September or October the glowing colours fade; the
annuals and biennials are a mess. The wheel barrow is piled high

with spent stems. It is sad, but also a relief, like tidying up a house after a riotous party. There is satisfaction in demolishing, clearing, forking the soil, sprinkling bone meal, and getting everything sober, dark and wholesome again, before planting out next year's wallflowers and foxgloves, hollyhocks and Canterbury bells in their allotted places.

VIII
The Ponds

A flat landscape with a big sky above calls for water. I set my heart on a pond – as big as possible, as natural-looking as possible, a sheet of water to reflect the clouds. After we had been here for three years, and could pretend to be at a loose end, my young son and I lifted turves and dug out a shape near the weeping willow trees, which were still alive; it was a simple curve with the ends pointing down the gentle slope, rather than up. We threw the earth into the concave shore of our curve, to make it look as though the water was forced to curve round a little mound. We wearied long before we had dug down the desired two feet, and a builder finished the job for us.

Whatever the do-it-yourself-in-the-garden books may say, ponds are tricky. If you want a big one, plastic sheeting may not do, and even concrete, which we chose, cracks in the end. Our pond was made with a little plug in the bottom, and a draining pipe running underground to the ditch, but after ten years it is only too ready to drain itself through its own hairline cracks and we have to fill it, periodically, with the garden hose. You have to do this in hot weather, anyway, as garden ponds evaporate at an astounding rate.

Nothing in a garden looks quite so glaringly unnatural as a newly-finished concrete pond. Ours sat there with its six-inch wide white kidney-shaped concrete edging gleaming in the rough grass. It was about twenty-seven feet long and eight feet wide, neither big nor tranquil – an absurdity. But I did not allow myself to see it as it was; you can train your vision to fix firmly on a dream of the future.

And water exercises a pull. You can sit beside it for a long time simply staring at it. It has a mixture of life and stillness which is mesmerising. We filled our hollow concrete shell with water and watched it change colour for a week and attract insects, until it was too dirty to be mesmerising at all (we were supposed to be 'seasoning the concrete'); then we pulled the plug and let out the first water and filled the pond up again with the second water, as the books advised.

Now the thrilling moment came. We arrived with a car-full of moist polythene packages, the results of evenings spent poring in rapture over Perry's catalogue of 'Water Lilies, Aquatic Plants and Hardy Fish'. Our packages, accordingly, were full of water lilies, aquatic plants and hardy fish, together with sets of special green plastic pots for standing under water, little ones for the oxygenating plants, big ones for the marginals and lilies. We pushed the plants into wet earth in the pots, and someone, dressed in a bathing costume, waded about placing them under water on the floor of the pond, at suitably random intervals.

How strange and fresh those 'submerged oxygenating aquatics' were — quite distinct from each other, some pale, some vivid, some ferny, some grass-like, some crisp as seaweed. How magic their promised powers sounded in the catalogue! Some sent up flowers to the surface of the water, some fed the fish, some were active during winter months. It was another world. We peered down through the water at them, standing in their little plastic pots; the water clouded, and soon we could see them no more. The following spring it was confirmed that most of them were dead.

The three water lily plants, rising from their larger pots, did better. They did not exactly prosper, but they managed to float their lily pads on the surface of the water and survive. One was *Nymphaea* × *marliacea* 'Carnea', blush-white; one was 'Rose Arey', blush-pink and starry; and one was 'James Brydon', rose-coloured with rounded cups of flowers floating flat upon the water.

The fish travelled in a huge bubble of polythene, pumped like a balloon with oxygen and with just a little water for them to rest on in the bottom. We suspended the balloon into the water

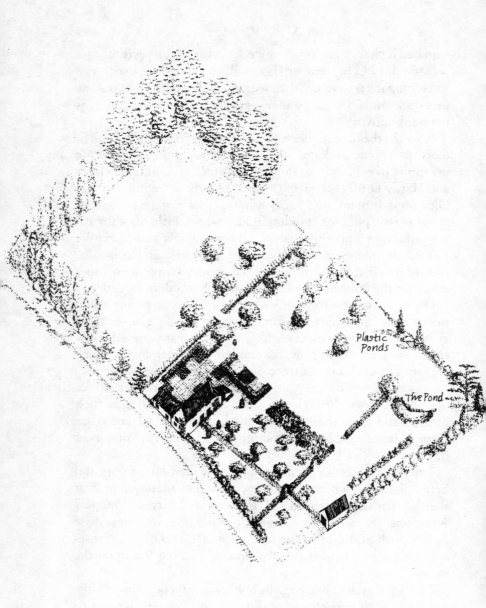

Plastic
Ponds

The Pond

The ponds.

over the edge of the pond, and when we judged the temperature to be right we released them into their large new home and they streaked away, a shoal of twelve tiny, streamlined golden orfe, each barely two inches long. Round and round the pond they raced; they loved to stick together. Gradually their numbers diminished; one dreadful day we saw a strange, multiple creature in the water; it was the deadly larva of a dragon-fly, and out of its mouth projected half a golden orfe. My youngest daughter wept; we all felt like crying.

We knew that it takes time to establish the correct balance between water, plants and fish in a garden pond; we were prepared to be patient; but the spring after the joyous May day on which we first planted our pond, with no orfe left and precious few plants, we decided to start again.

We salvaged the lilies, some marginals and the two remaining oxygenators, and stood their pots in tubs and buckets of water while we drained the pond again. We then set to work with spades and shovels and covered the entire floor of the pond with soil, to a depth of three or four inches. Into this we planted our survivors, and gradually we ran fresh water in again.

It worked – I don't know why; perhaps our pond was just too big for the other, pot-plant method; now the plants grew prodigiously, as if to show they had been insulted by the artificiality of plastic pots. The water became clear, and dark, just as it should. We bought a new collection of fish – gold-fish this time, and shubunkins as well as orfe; most of them prospered. We could sit on a white iron seat beside the water and wait for them to surface from the dark depths under the lily pads when we threw them food. We gave them names and grew familiar with them.

One curly, many-stemmed oxygenator took over: *Elodea crispa*; it ramps through the water and now we have to remove great rakesful of it every spring. (It makes a useful mulch.) It is probably too vigorous to be let loose in a pond, but we would rather have an over-vigorous oxygenator than feeble ones that die.

The water lilies ramp now, too, except for 'James Brydon', which has finally been ousted by the other two. That is the trouble with ponds; water is a life-giver and plants that grow in it multiply; when a pond works, it works too well. All our extant water plants exploited the freedom we gave them in the mud on the pool's floor; we have to tear up the mighty water lily pads by their long, rubbery stems if we are to have so much as a patch of clear water left to show us the fish and reflect the sky. If we are not careful the water lily flowers, instead of floating, rise up above the water on three-inch stems, jostling for space, and so do the lily pads. One must be vigilant every spring, ruthless with the rake. And one must keep a constant watch for slimy blanket weed and rake it out too. To achieve a balanced pond is an anxious matter; to keep it is a constant battle.

The fish breed too; unsavoury brown ones appear in great numbers in the spring-time (where the first one came from, we do not know). We kept most of our shubunkin for several years; they seemed hardier than the gold fish, though less beautiful; our pond was large enough to supply them with food in the long weeks when we were not there to feed them, and in the winter we left a rubber ball floating on the surface to prevent it freezing over and depriving the fish of air. In the summer, we would feel a sudden joy in seeing old friends reappear from under the newly sprouting lilies; if it is possible to waste time staring at water, it is possible to waste hours of time watching for fish.

But we have been visited by herons; once, returning from a day's outing on a summer evening, we glimpsed one standing like a garden ornament at one end of the pond; we took several seconds to adjust our reaction, to see through its breath-taking beauty to the horror of its intentions; it ate several of our friends. Another time we saw a heron flying across the sky. Soon after that, all our fish were gone. We bought a big roll of green plastic netting and spread it right over the pond in winter, when the herons are most hungry, fastening it into the surrounding beds with stakes. It never quite reaches round one awkward corner. In very icy weather, if one walks towards the pond, there may be a sudden beating of great wings and the heron rises slowly above us from behind the hedge, leaving us as aghast at his presence as he must be at ours. We are thinking of trying that frightful indignity, a large plastic heron, to stand near the vulnerable corner of the pond in winter.

The floor of our pond slopes upwards at either end; it was in the shallows at one end that the heron stood. And in those shallows we originally placed our other pots, containing plants that do best in a few inches of water: *Iris laevigata*, the blue one and the white, and *Butomus umbellatus*, the flowering rush, with huge pink globular heads composed of many tiny flowerets like an allium or onion flower, but much more beautiful, lovely even in death. These are all still standing there in their pots today, though no doubt their roots have penetrated through the pots and are fastened in the mud by now; indeed, the flowering reed has seeded itself, and now forms a handsome and prodigal clump at just the right place in the centre of the curving, convex bank – it looks more beautiful in its chance position, in deep water, than it does in its official one. These marginal plants help the pond to look natural and to mask its concrete edges.

For the biggest problem of all with our pond was its concrete edge. The soil beside a concrete pond is no damper than the soil anywhere else in the garden, unless the pond is leaking, and therefore the delectable, moisture-loving plants that should spread in the firm soil at the margin and then sprawl over the edge and spread out in the water will very likely fail to prosper, unless you are there to water them all the time. Our water forget-me-not, *Myosotis palustris*, flourished for a year, then dwindled; we had only very partial success with another delightful, blue-flowering marginal, brooklime, and the marsh marigold, *Caltha palustris*, was a dead loss. The plants that have agreed to clothe our concrete are, ironically, dry soil and sun lovers: creeping thyme, *Thymus serpyllum*, and catmint. But the plant that really rejoices in that edging, and seems to draw sustenance from the very concrete itself, is couch grass.

By now, however, the concrete edge no longer seems to worry us; perhaps we have got used to it; its colour is much better, duller; it has weathered; it is almost like stone. We have encouraged moss to grow upon it by painting it with milk and, most important of all, we have paved one whole curving side of the pond, the side where we sit, with old slabs of stone, salvaged from an excavation in a London basement garden. Paving and a garden pond go well together; when we grew grass right up to the edge, we could not mow it, and had to manicure the fringe by hand, and watch the cut grass fall into the water. Now, on one side of our pond at least, the couch grass is defeated; on the other side, a valiant bank of obliging, lovely *Iris sibirica* struggles with the couch for dominance, and may one day be victorious.

Indeed, we have flower beds right round our pond and paving now; the beds extend the lines of the curve at each end and carry on a little way down the slope. Thick and luxurious planting helps all but the most formal pond to look settled. In a fit of romanticism, and influenced by a photograph of a beautiful mill house in a magazine, I planted musk roses near the water at each end – musk rose 'Felicia', almost as pale pink as the water lilies themselves, and bowing low over the water to meet them. The petals fall into the water, which is bad, for rotting vegetation clouds the pond; nor can one ever spray the roses, for fear of poisoning the fish; but they do look pretty, and they have survived. So too has one tall moisture-loving plant survived: the wonderfully choice *Rodgersia pinnata* 'Superba', with large green palmate leaves and a strong yet subtle spire of dull red flowers, the sort of flower-stem that justifies and gives point to an otherwise dull flower arrangement – and, once picked, the stem slowly dries itself, and remains shapely and handsome for months.

Now, in May, there is a new excitement; having failed to raise foxtail lilies from seed, and admired them to distraction in an

Essex garden where they were liberally planted in a formal setting, I have bought three bulbs of *Eremurus elwesii* and planted them to mark the far point of the border below the pond. Even the first year, they rose to their astonishing height of seven feet; it is the mixture of height with unsupportedness that holds the eye; there is a mere mat of basal leaves, then the long, slim stem topped by an equally long, slim poker of pink/white flowers. A lily pond is a study in the horizontal plane; perhaps that is why the foxtail lilies look right beside it – an unequalled celebration of the vertical.

By chance, most of the other things that grow in the pond-side beds look well, too, and a sort of gentle colour scheme is beginning to assert itself, though not so absolutely as to be tyrannical; it derives from some good, fortuitous plant-associations. A hump of rue, 'Jackman's Blue', grows beside a clump of *Iris pallida* 'Variegata', the rather fashionable and delightful iris with glaucous leaves striped in cream and a fleeting blue iris flower; beyond grows a healthy patch of white double daisies, *Chrysanthemum maximum* 'Wirral Supreme', flowering in July and August; and beyond these, patches of lacy, wiry thalictrum, ferny green, and *Astrantia major*, green pin-cushion flowers with a blush of pink; then the huge stems of the silver scotch thistle, *Onopordum acanthium*. Further on there are tufts of the blue grass, *Festuca glauca*, then a luxurious round shrub of the rugosa rose 'Alba', chalk-white flowers all summer and hips of tomato red; then the blue-green pleated leaves of *Hosta sieboldiana*; then a thicket of tall, pale green bamboos; then the tall but gently drooping leaves of the wild flag iris. And so I discover that mainly white flowers, with some green ones, mixed with many pale shades of leaf from glaucous blue to gold and silver, look peaceful round the pond, and prettier than bright flowers would do.

I have discovered too, in the course of a search for extra space, that certain unlikely vegetables look at home in the pond-side beds: sweet corn, with its rushy maize leaves, planted in groups of four or five for better fertilisation, looks as good as any ornamental grass; and globe artichokes, whose grey-green leaves are in sympathy with the scotch thistle, have petalled buds as delectable as any exotic green flower before we eat them, and if we fail to eat them, huge, honey-scented flowers of an intoxicating blue.

By chance and faith, rather than by forethought and good management, our pond is now something we need not be ashamed of. But not without a further, major hitch.

About twelve years after it was made, its hairline cracks began to widen. The leak was obvious. It was never more than half full. Should we fill the whole thing in with soil and call a halt to water gardening? Such a suggestion made me realise how much I valued it. Should we buy a vast and costly heavy-duty plastic liner and try to camouflage the edges where it would overlap the paving? First we would see what we could do ourselves, with paintbrushes and seals. We spent dedicated summer days transplanting the lilies and the water irises into plastic containers in the ditch; we shovelled out all the soppy mud, full of old water lily tubers, spreading it over flower beds in the belief that it must be good, rich stuff, however awful it looked; we then washed and scrubbed the surface of the concrete with the help of a wire brush, a stiff broom, and a hose. And then we set to work in earnest. We filled the serious cracks with mastic, reinforced with twists of kitchen foil wherever these could be poked in. We painted the entire surface of the pond four times over with heavy-duty water proofing. We crossed our fingers and rigged up the hose. It took two hours just to cover the deepest bit of the floor with water. I kept going back to look, watching bits of dry bamboo leaf and a rose leaf with black spot on it circling. Two hours later a brilliant dragonfly was darting about, its shimmering blue and green were the colour of rue leaves and alchemilla flowers, and beautiful as a peacock's blue and green. 'Please let this dragonfly be an augury of a continuing pond,' I prayed. next morning it was full. We turned off the tap and left it for the winter. In the spring it was still brim full. We let out the water and arranged new soil over the bottom – sparingly this time, with a view to future shovelling should the whole sequence repeat itself in some nightmare future. We rescued our brave water plants from the wretched puddles where they had been clinging onto life, and we replanted the best of them in the new soil. We filled up again with water, and the water lilies grew and spread out as if nothing had happened. That was four years ago. It seems too good to be true. Once more we sit on the white iron seat by the water, and watch our new fish darting between our old water lilies.

There was a time, before this strenuous episode, when I thought I would like more ponds. I had realised, a year or two after it was originally dug, that our pond was wrongly sited – we had impulsively excavated a likely corner, guided by those diseased weeping willows. Though the willows have gone, we have made the site look all right, through subsequent plantings; you approach it through an arch in a hedge, and reach it as the focal point of a further, 'secret' garden. But that is not how gardens should develop; you should not have to 'make things all right' as you go along; and it is now quite clear where the water in our garden ought to be: it ought to be at the lowest point, in the ditch that separates the bottom of the garden from the field. It should lie between the two fastigiate beeches that frame our view. It should be shaped like a canal, long and narrow, like a little strip of moat, or a trapped stream; if it were there, one could believe that it had always been there.

Once more my son (much older now) and I sprang into action. We could not cope with concreting, but I reasoned that a series of little rectangular, ready-made plastic ponds, bought at the local water nurseries and sunk into the ditch by my son, end to end, could give the main idea with comparatively little trouble; we would space the pools out like beads on a string, and we would plant the little bridges of earth between them with all those marginals that had failed to prosper by the concrete pond.

From this exploit we learnt at least two things: first, it is not at all easy to settle those rigid, ready-made pools into the ground. We worked hard at it, with lots of gusto and a spirit level; the pools had very curious contours underneath, steps and ripples, designed to accommodate plants of different requirements; we attempted to make the earth of our ditch into a sort of mirror reflection of these contours, like a plaster mould; with a good deal of trial and error we got three grey plastic rectangles into line, sunk more or less at the same level into our ditch, and we filled them with pond water from our dear old established pond so as to avoid the remembered horror of algae forming in fresh tap water. Immediately we got lovely reflections of the sky, and the water never clouded; we had a little earth in the bottom and planted a few new aquatics; but the grey plastic edges of the four rectangles looked, of course, monstrous, and as the weeks went by and the ponds settled, ominous frills and scallops began to form in those edges, augurs of cracks to come. We planted our remaining scraps of water forget-me-not and brooklime, as planned, on the bridges between the rectangles, and I hopefully arranged a row of 'pamments', tiles and bricks along the sides in an amateurish attempt to mask them. But not the most resolute visionary could see those little ponds as anything of permanent significance in the landscape; we tried to avoid showing visitors this bit of the garden, though one, exploring alone, returned to ask: 'What are those tanks at the bottom of the lawn?'

7 a) **The pond**: beyond the galtonias in bud and the arching wands of the giant Scotch thistle, *Onopordum acanthium*, lies the pond, with its pink and white water lilies and its pale striped grass (*Glyceria maxima* 'Variegata'). *Rosa rugosa* 'Alba' is mustering its second flush of flowers behind the iron seat.

7 b) **The vegetable garden**: the courgette flowers amid its marbled leaves, and beyond are tomatoes, French beans, parsnips and a ferny forest of asparagus. Clipped beech hedges serve instead of walls to give warmth and shelter to the crops.

After a year, the original situation was reversed; the pleasant water was all gone from two out of the three ponds – the pressure of the water against the imperfectly bedded, flimsy plastic had caused cracks, and they were ponds no more. We should have dug deeper, bedded them in sand; I should not have put sharp and heavy stones along the sides. On the other hand, the edges went too, disappearing beneath a lush growth of marginals; indeed, the absurd, dimpled grey insides of our pools were now clothed in the natural prettiness of thriving forget-me-not and starry, deeper blue brooklime, effortlessly taking the prefabricated plastic contours and making them natural; a clump of moisture-loving grass, *Glyceria maxima* 'Variegata', which never flourished by the concrete, spread here – gracing the ditch with its cream-striped leaves.

We also learnt, before the water seeped away, the beauty of our new aquatics: the pickerel weed, *Pontederia cordata*, water hawthorn, *Aponogeton distachyas*, which we planted instead of water lilies as being more modestly suitable to the small pools; we were charmed by its sprays of fresh white flowers with black anthers, held a little above the water, as by its pretty, lozenge-shaped leaves floating flat on the water's surface. One day, we must make another home for it.

We used those leaky plastic pools as homes for our lilies while we mended the concrete pond; they served their turn. With some satisfaction, we have at last wrenched them out of the ditch and burned them. Three curiously moulded cavities remain behind them, marking where they were.

If we hired a digger and dug a much deeper, wider, natural ditch down there, might the water stay in it all the year round? I know it wouldn't, but I long to try.

8 **Early morning on the fen**: at 7.30 one August morning, after weeks of cloud and rain, the sun came through the clouds and shone across polygonum and salvia, helenium and achillea in the border and touched the silver willow beyond.

IX

The Bulbs and the Wood

Daffodils: brave, beloved flowers that dance in the wind and bob up again even after they've bowed low in snow – the very word 'daffodil' is enough to evoke spring, and renewal, and the English country garden. But there are two, well-known provisos which I took to heart: first, the daffodils must not be planted out tamely in flower beds, where their leaves will be a nuisance for two months after the flowers die, and where their bulbs will be vulnerable to the border fork when the leaves, too, are gone; they must be naturalised in grass; second, the daffodils must come in dozens, in scores, in hundreds; it was quantity that caught Wordsworth's eye:

> 'Ten thousand saw I at a glance,
> Tossing their heads in sprightly dance.'

I saw them, from the first, as an obvious means of bringing poetry to our dull plot in the Easter holidays. I could almost say that we planted our first fruit trees so that daffodils would grow in the grass beneath them. I had once visited an Elizabethan farmhouse in Sussex in April and seen, through the dining room window, groups of daffodils in different colours, white and yellow, growing in the grass under apple trees on a gentle, rising slope. From this I learnt that I did not like all yellow, or all white, as much as I liked them mixed; even in spring-time, even with daffodils, one can have a surfeit of gold. (And all-white would be perverse, at daffodil time.) I liked trumpet daffodils mixed with flat-faced ones, double with single, orange centred with pale centred; I liked short, early daffodils and late, elegant narcissi – I liked them all, and like to have them blooming for the whole possible extent of the daffodil season, that is from February or March to May. For six weeks, if there are enough of them, they alone will carry the garden.

But of course, the vision in the inward eye takes years to realise. We started with about two dozen bulbs, and duly scattered them, in our first autumn, round the areas where our brand-new, tiny fruit trees were to go. I still remember my half-acknowledged disappointment the next spring: the gap between vision and reality was too wide to bridge; each of our bulbs seemed to produce only one flower (I suppose they were cheap, single bulbs) and, again for purposes of economy, we had spaced the bulbs quite far apart, and the fact was that they made no sort of effect at all, dotted thinly in the still rough grasses, under the almost invisible, neatly-staked apple trees – no more uplifting than the odd dandelion dotted in a lawn.

But daffodil bulbs do multiply, given reasonable soil; each single bulb will, over the years, become a cluster; rain, in the all-important season when the flowers are over but the leaves still grow, hastens the process; we had a series of dry springs, but gradually came the desired effect: bunches of daffodils, nine or ten identical flowers together, growing in smooth green grass. They know how to arrange themselves as if held, loosely, in a sympathetic flower-arranger's fist, trumpets pointing outwards, all round the group. They lean away from each other just enough for each to be distinct, while yet a group, and their leaves, perfectly behaved because a little shorter than the flowers at first, are essential to their beauty; the cool blue in the green of a daffodil leaf is the corrective to too much yellow.

And so, as with all our gardening effects, patience was needed. We resolved that each year we would plant more bulbs, as many as we could afford, as many as we had time to plant, and they would gradually thicken. At first we bought them from posh catalogues; later, by the pound weight, in cheap batches from the market. From the experts we bought old-fashioned, early daffodils: the little Tenby daffodil, ten inches high on a sturdy stem to withstand the March winds (*Narcissus pseudo-narcissus obvallaris*), its classic trumpet like a miniature 'King

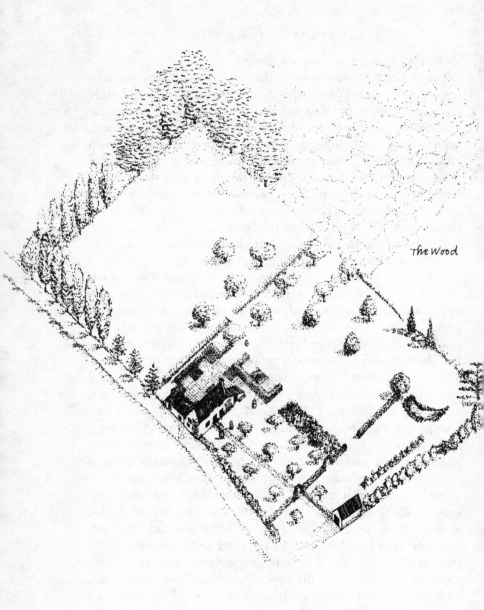

The Wood

We expand into the wood.

Alfred', or a child's picture of a daffodil; and its faithful ten inch cousin, 'Van Sion', muddle-centred and scrambled, the original double daffodil; it is not elegant, it is cottagey and a sterling doer. I grow these small, early daffodils near the house, where we can see them without going out of doors. The more popular, deservedly famous cyclamineus hybrid, 'February Gold', is, for me in cold East Anglia, usually a March daffodil too, though it is always the first to open and has a lasting power second to none; it blooms for at least four weeks, and is an abundant flowerer, its flowers less classic than Tenby's, with delicate, slightly reflexed petals that have an air of flight about them.

My favourite mid-season daffodil is 'John Evelyn', with an ivory-white perianth and short, frilled apricot cup; though recommended to me as a spreader, mine is rather shy, which may be partly why I treasure it. My mid-season spreaders and standbys are the three daffodils that come in the market mixtures: 'Carlton', an absolutely reliable yellow trumpet, just a little paler than 'King Alfred' and all the better for it; 'Mount Hood', a cream trumpet, fading to white; and 'Sempre avanti', a flatter-faced narcissus with deep cream perianth and flaming orange centre. Many other daffodils may come in those mixed bags as well; most of my beauties are nameless to me.

The later bloomers, however, are easily recognisable; the two polyanthus narcissi 'Cheerfulness', the yellow and the white, with their clusters of small, heavily-scented double flowers, three or four to a single stem; and the even more divinely scented poeticus narcissi, including the old May-flowering 'Pheasant's Eye', pure white with its eye of gold, red-rimmed. I grow the white narcissi under the white cherry blossom, which also flowers in May.

Daffodils are for picking, in great armsful, and for admiring out of windows. Our first plantations were not ideally placed; the groups under the apple trees happen to be in the line our dog takes when dashing to bark at a neighbouring Alsatian. It is an agony to watch the flowers fall during one of these charges, though the vases in the house can be kept filled with casualties, which saves the alternative pain of cutting flowers that look perfect out of doors; and if the picked flowers come in varying lengths – for dogs are not consistent in their breaking of stems, then the resulting bunch will look the prettier. There is nothing more deadly to arrange than a florist's bunch of a dozen identical, even-stemmed, monochrome daffodils.

Our other original drift, under the cherry trees, is now completely obscured from the house windows by the yew hedge. I sat at the table under the kitchen window in April and saw that I must begin to extend my daffodil plantings so that we could see them from the kitchen table where we ate. We now have daffodils right down the ditch, on both sides, and spreading up two mounds, made of dumped garden rubbish, where the ditch meets the wood. As I said at the beginning, daffodils look specially good if allowed to climb up little slopes.

This wood is a later addition to our garden, a third of an acre of wilderness. We bought it from the neighbouring poultry farmer when he finally moved away; it is the overgrown patch of ground that lay to the south of our field. Two decaying weatherboard sheds stood on it, and when the farm closed down the vegetation swiftly took over – not the rank weeds of our original plot, but woody stuff seeding from the tall trees and hedgerow that surrounded this small tongue of land. One side had become a little thicket of elder, its dead twigs brittle underfoot; otherwise there were odd saplings of hawthorn and ash, the whole bound together with mighty arching wands of bramble and roped with twining hops. The carpeting was nettles. We fought battles with the brambles and often lost; there is still a lot of bramble there. We slashed at some of the elder bushes, which in certain moods we tend to regard as weeds. We have cut some elder down to ground level and soused it with brushwood killer, but up it comes again. Now that we have a delicious recipe for elderflower cordial, we are reluctant to eradicate it altogether. We pulled the two sheds down but otherwise we have done little to the wood apart from trying to encourage it to become more so; when, after the spraying and slashing, some parts of it looked quite bare, we became wood-men, and wandered about moving saplings from crowded spots to empty spots; we stuck branches of willow into the ground and hoped they'd take; we planted a pink flowered hawthorn as a minor excitement amongst the native white. We also planted an alder, whose seedheads and catkins adorn vases of winter twigs and make an unassuming framework in a jug of daffodils in spring. Rather more grandly, we planted a red oak, *Quercus rubra*, for the sake of its reliably brilliant autumn colour, but it is nothing like as happy as the little sprouting English acorns we move into the wood from other places. Finally, we moved an *Amelanchier lamarckii*, the 'Snowy mespilus', from somewhere else, and hope that in a half-shady place it will still produce its starry white flowers and its rich autumn reds.

Meanwhile, the ash saplings grew. Ash, that stately tree, that source of excellent firewood, seeds itself with generosity in this patch of ground, perhaps because it is both moist and sandy. Here, if you dig down far enough, you come to white sand, and below the sand, to water; you are on the fen. Once upon a time, it seems, this was the bed of a lake; all these self-seeding trees are the sort that enjoy getting their roots into the wetness that lies only a few feet down. Whatever sows itself here, looks right; whatever I plant, tends to look wrong. We once stuck a left-over Christmas tree with a bit of root on it into the wood and it is still growing, but looks a fright. Extreme tact is needed when it comes to gardening in a wood. Nature is boss here.

But it is fun to try to tame her, gently, and if you do it sensibly, she rewards you. When we cleared the nettles, she rewarded us with sheets of wild forget-me-nots the next spring; where it is very dark under the elders, she supplied a carpet of ivy, pierced by lords and ladies, those strange, furled bracts like pale green lilies, with their later stems of sealing-wax red berries. And where light filters through, herb Robert came, a lacy thing with delicate pink flowers that is sometimes called poor Robin. Then honesty, blowing down from an attempted takeover in the herb garden, set up its healthy colonies.

Nature plants in sheets; that is what 'naturalising' means; it implies multiplication. I have planted single things in the wood and, though they have survived, nature has not adopted them and they have not, therefore, 'naturalised'. Here a single primrose, here a single bluebell, there – some lonely leaves of pulmonaria beneath a hawthorn, a single clump of flag irises beside a boggy dip in the ground: all these look accidental. I persevere. The cranesbill, *Geranium grandiflorum*, is a tough customer. I have seen it on rough shady banks in other people's gardens. And as I am banishing it from favoured flower borders where it is getting out of hand (it spreads greedily on good soil) I am making plantations of it here in the wood. The sad alternative would be to throw it on the compost heap. Its wide blue saucer flowers and pretty leaves would be warmly welcome.

Lily of the valley – why should I do without it? I have dug it a bed here beneath an ash tree in dappled shade – six feet by six feet – conscientiously pulling out great horizontal ropes of roots and burying half-rotted leaf-mould in their place. As things go in this wood, it is not a bad bed. I have ordered fifty plants and plan to set them very close together. If they flourish, I shall introduce some Solomon's seal behind them, to arch over them.

Ferns, too, are tempting. I have planted two – *Polystichum setiferum* 'Divisilobum', with prettily cut, lacy fronds as its name suggests, and a marsh buckler fern, sent by a gardening friend. They look like alien episodes, side by side, each in its own small clearing amongst the ivy, but if either of them should choose to naturalise it will be a different matter. My knowledgeable friend has sent me other vernal things: *G. macrophyllum*, with large, handsome leaves, and a native rush – *Luzula sylvatica* 'Marginata'; surely the rush at least, a lover of dry shade, will quickly look at home.

Meanwhile I have one triumph: snowdrops. I had planted snowdrops outside our boundary hedge, beside the gate; but when we acquired the wood, I knew I would like them there as well. I bought some snowdrops from a nursery that sends them out in spring 'in green', for it is said that, at this moment, when they have finished flowering but still have their leaves, they transplant best. And so it proved. I planted at least fifty little bulbs, fairly close together, in imitation of one of Nature's sheets, digging my trowel into the already root-infested earth for I was too hasty to undertake what those who write of 'wild gardening' advise: that is, to dig the beds at first, and cultivate the wilderness until the new plants 'take'. However, for once I had been generous enough with my original planting to get an effect: the snowdrops came up ever more thickly every year in their appointed place; they would not, however, seed themselves about, so I stepped in and moved them with my trowel. The original sheet was altogether too thick now to be convincing, considering that there were no snowdrops anywhere else in the wood, and so I have become a self-appointed naturaliser and am dividing the clumps 'in green' each spring – a delightful occupation which my family calls 'exercising the plants' and which has something in common with 'doing the flowers'.

'Where would another little clump of snowdrops look nice?' I ask myself. 'Over *there*? Or here?' The answer is: *everywhere*. And so the little colonies are placed, in an ever-widening area round the parent plantation every spring. The following spring they obediently reappear; their tiny leaves have the same satisfying colour as a daffodil's, and protect the flowers in the same touching way; the flowers themselves are the perfection of simplicity. I do not hanker after large snowdrops, rare snowdrops; I grow the common one of the woods, *Galanthus nivalis*; I suppose it is accommodating itself so well to our wood because it is a woodland flower; yet nothing could be more delicate; it has a linear property which asks to be drawn, a simple shape when closed, a shape like a fairy's white skirts with a scalloped, green-hemmed petticoat when open. Close to the ground, myriads of tiny white specks amongst last year's dead twigs and the lichened stems of trees, my snowdrops spread through the wood now and catch the eye with an unaccountably moving promise of spring.

When spring is past, Nature takes over in the wood, and summer is a tangle of cow parsley followed by hops. We keep a path cut, looping through the clearings of the wood, by periodically bumping along it on the ride-on mower. A grass path, leading between banks of leafy shade, is inviting. To make this path we had to cut things down, a few at first, then more, as the idea of a vista took hold. We used to look from our kitchen window down into the wood's leafiness; in winter we could see through it, but in summer it was nothing but a wall of deep green shadow, almost two-dimensional. I made the vista very gingerly at first, in the face of conservative opposition.

'You will spoil it.'

'You'll *ruin* it.'

'You will take away the secrecy.'

'We don't want a vista.'

But now it is there, and it has made a third dimension and a real, framed view. At the vista's end, the nicest tree in the wood, an old hedgerow oak, flings out a cradling branch to frame a tunnel-like view into the meadow beyond. The path curves and divides, and along its sides we plant, each autumn, more and more daffodils.

I have a new idea for the edges of this woodland path: *Rosa eglanteria*, the sweet briar. It is classified as one of the roses that will put up with partial shade and anyway its delicious scent comes not from its flowers, but from its fresh young leaves. I shall put two or three bushes just behind the daffodils and amongst the cow parsley – I know it will look right here for there is already a leggy, pale pink dog rose in the wood, fighting for life in a dark corner between an elder and a hawthorn, strayed in from the meadow's hedgerows.

The wood is flat. The garden slopes down to it. I have given the impression that the grass path extends a little way up into the garden by devising two long, tapering beds that break the straight boundary line of the wood, like promontories, and carry woodland plantings in them. They are not just flower beds, or they would not do the trick of looking like extensions of the wood; there are two young pear trees in one: 'Doyenné de Comice' and 'Beurre Superfin', and the winter flowering cherry, *Prunus subhirtella* 'Autumnalis', flings wide its delicate, spreading branches in the other. Beside it a red stemmed dogwood, *Cornus alba* 'Sibirica', looks good in winter and is cut down hard in spring. The grass path runs between these beds and all the things that would not prosper in the wood have been transplanted and grow along it. *Pulmonaria officinalis* or lungwort, lost among the undergrowth, flourished here, its spotted leaves only less handsome than its intense blue and pink flowers; lilies (*Lilium henryi*), too exotic an event among the lords and ladies, looked at home here; so did hellebores, *Euphorbia epithymoides* (short stemmed and spring flowering, with acid green flowers) tradescantias, *Astrantia* (the masterwort, with greenish white pincushion flowers) and foxgloves. And here I hit upon a really successful plant association: foxgloves and columbines, both grown from seed and seeding themselves thereafter. The strains I used – 'Foxy' for the foxgloves and Sutton's long-spurred hybrids for the columbines, used the same palette of colours, cream, pale yellow, pale pink, with occasional hints of mauve or blue. The delight was to see these same colours embodied in such differently shaped flowers – the foxgloves with tall and stately spikes, the little dangling 'glove tips' fat, spotted and loveable; the columbines frail and pastel, with exquisitely poised fly-away flowers, and the two together complementing each other, the fat and the frail flowering at the same time. Primroses, too, prospered here along the edges of the borders, a breathtaking strain of Barnhaven primroses with huge, scented faces, some primrose yellow, some white. I often fail to divide them until the autumn, but still they prosper and increase. Amongst them grow colonies of *Anemone blanda*, with even bigger faces, like thrilling saxe-blue daisies mixed with a few pinks and whites. Forget-me-not has come, uninvited, to join the spring carpet, and so has ornithogalum, the Star of Bethlehem, and little mauve violets, unannounced. I have added snakeshead fritillaries, hanging their inimitable chequered bells in shades of wine, pale green and cream. They are shy, hiding between other plants, both wild-looking and exquisite. All these small things carpet the beds in April and, though the foxgloves and columbines rule in June, the bulbs and spreaders are so lovely that these borders are called 'the spring garden'.

Most bulbs are easy: easy to plant, easy to place. Nearly all my most successful placings in this garden turn out to have bulbs as a component. There are two, symmetrical groups of crown imperials, *Fritillaria imperialis*, at the further end of two parallel herb garden beds. Every April up they come, stiff and straight, thicker each year – daffodil yellow and thus perfectly attuned to the banks of daffodils glimpsed beyond them. They are regal in stance, impervious to winds, and should be planted as features, to stand alone, or towering over shorter neighbours. Their crowns are startling topknots of green, and from these the jewels drop downwards, a complete circlet of large yellow bells which open wider and wider as the generous weeks of their flowering go by. As soon as they come through the earth in spring, their strange acrid smell warns of their arrival, and permeates every part of the plant; in the dormant season, if a trowel touches the bulbs below ground, the fierce smell will warn you to dig no further. By happy chance, my clumps are viewed against a background of yew hedge beyond them; I did not know, when I first stuck them in, that they would always be seen against a yew-dark background. Now I have planted two clumps of the other crown imperial, the tawny orange coloured one, on either side of the gap in our southern hedge, for clumps of crown imperials should be arranged, I now know, in complementary pairs. The globular alliums flower in summer: *Allium albopilosum* (now *A. christophii*) in June, with strong, slender stems eighteen inches high, on top of which open the ten-inch spheres of lilac-coloured flowers; their wiry, almost metallic starriness offsets the softness of old roses, as visitors to the rose garden at Sissinghurst know well. *Allium aflatunense* is earlier and less spectacular, a quarter the size, and a rather vulgar mauve, the colour of chives flowers, but it is a faithful doer, and when one suddenly appeared behind a mass of rosy mauve aubretia, I discovered that this was where it looked best, its bare stem rising out of soft mats of aubretia in the same colours. When the aubretia finishes flowering, and has to be shorn, the allium seed-heads remain, pale buff, stiff and beautiful, awaiting the flower arranger's scissors.

In late June the madonna lilies reign; they used to grow in the herbaceous border, which proved an inadequate setting for their purity. They, like crown imperials, need to stand alone. I made narrow beds for them along the edges of the concrete slab which covers the septic tank, and planted them barely below the level of the earth; they look now as if they are growing out of the grass. Between them stands the terracotta Italian vase, and when they flower round it they form a composition like an incident in the corner of an Annunciation by a Renaissance painter. They are multiplying now that they are allowed to stand alone; nothing is as white, waxy and divinely scented as their flowers.

But regal lilies (*Lilium regale*) run them a close second: their perfume is heavier, more sophisticated, their waxy white is tinged with rose at the back, along the veins. For all their handsome stature, they do well in pots; I have planted some in two old coppers, the colour of verdigris, pushing the wine-red bulbs, as many-lobed as a globe artichoke, quite deeply into enriched potting compost, where I plan to leave them undisturbed.

In August the Cape hyacinths, *Galtonia candicans*, bring back spring freshness translated into a glamorous late summer flower. You would expect this glorious, graceful bulb to be tender or tricky, but it is not; its white bells dangle like blown-up snowflakes, clustered round the two-foot stem like the hyacinth flowret suggested in its alternative name, *Hyacinthus candicans*. It quietly dominates a bed beside the pond ·in summer, and makes an important, tall, cut flower.

Down at the bottom of the garden, as August fades into September, the 'naked ladies', *Colchicum autumnale*, suddenly appear. They are 'naked' because they have no leaves at flowering time; their fragile, hollow white stems (strictly speaking their perianth tube) merge and swell into lilac-pink crocus-like chalices, but they are bigger and pinker than any crocus. Nearby flower the autumn cyclamen, *Cyclamen neapolitanum*, tiny replicas of the potted cyclamen of Christmas presents and florists' shops, adorable pink miniatures, the same colour as the colchicums, happy to grow amongst the fallen needles round the skirts of the cedar tree. In spring leaves come up: the colchicum's are large and bright, to make up for the fragility of the flowers; the cyclamen's are a little like ivy leaves, but exquisitely marbled. I bought my cyclamen from a nursery that sends them out in spring 'in green'; in this way, it is easy to know which side up to plant the otherwise inscrutable corms.

In late September and October comes another happy bulb association for I have planted nerines, *Nerine bowdenii*, beneath 'Zéphirine Drouhin', the climbing rose by the front door. The nerines take a year or two to settle down and multiply, and need a sheltered spot, but once they are established, they delight every autumn with the improbably fresh pink of their amaryllis flowers, which matches the flush of intense pink in the autumn roses. More and more, it is matching, rather than contrasting flowers, that give a subtle pleasure.

In October the autumn crocuses should be flowering; I have planted scores of the beautiful easy one, *Crocus speciosus*, blue laced with a network of deeper blue veins, with a bright saffron stigmata in the centre of its cup. They never survive for long. One or two flower for a year, perhaps, then disappear. An old wives' tale has led me to plant reinforcement crocus bulbs with prickly old holly leaves all round them in the holes I dig for them in the turf; a painful technique which will prove worth it if it keeps the mice away. At present the mice eat the bulbs before the sparrows get a turn at the flowers. But the great crocus grower, H. E. Bowles, promises us that the autumn crocus will spread through self-seeding as well as bulb-splitting until it is almost as difficult to eradicate from a garden as ground elder. He advises early planting. I shall try once more for those imagined sheets of autumn blue.

It is the same story with the species crocuses of early spring. I'm lucky if I get half a dozen silvery mauve *Crocus tomasinianus* and three clumps of creamy *Crocus chrysanthus* growing in the grass. I have to shrug my shoulders, and look forward to the daffodils.

X

The Shrubs and the Roses

Flowering shrubs, the standbys of the modern garden, did not at first seem of importance here, where trees, hedges and herbaceous plants were giving the place its shape. But one by one, over the years, the flowering shrubs have suggested themselves to fill gaps – gaps in the garden and gaps in the year. Slowly and steadily they have come marching in in their black plastic, easily-transported, utterly tempting pots; the only way to resist them is to resist visiting the garden centres that now lure gardeners, all over England, to load trolleys with serve-yourself plants as if they were casual groceries.

At first we chose late summer-flowering shrubs, flowers for July and August; then we planted winter-flowerers, shrubs for Christmas and the bleak New Year; then we began to feel a serious lack of autumn colour in our apple- and willow-dominated garden, and looked for shrubs whose leaves turn red before they fall. And now, I buy the odd shrub here and there because I find it irresistible.

In this last category, four shrubs spring to mind: *Cytisus* × *praecox*, inconspicuously neat for most of the year, but breathtaking in April, when it flowers all over its low mound and is a cascade of cream flowers along weeping branches; ours weeps among a circle of 'February Gold' daffodils. All you have to do to ensure this display which makes you catch your breath as at a rocket or cartwheel or fountain firework suspended in the air is to cut it back all over as soon as it has flowered. (Its strongly acrid scent does not match its sweet appearance.)

Second comes another breathtaking cytisus: *C. battandieri*, whose glory is its pineapple-scented racemes of golden flowers in June/July. I first saw it as a towering wall shrub in full flower on someone else's grand, south-facing wall. When I saw it next,

at a garden centre, I bought it. I have no house wall for it, but it grows against a wall of clipped leylandii instead, spreading out its silver-satin, three-lobed leaves, its long stems trained to bamboo stakes. It has survived the severest of winters, and is growing at full speed.

My third irresistible shrub is *Viburnum plicatum tomentosum* 'Lanarth' variety – that spectacularly spreading thing which needs space round it if it is to be seen in its full symmetrical stateliness, with plates of white flowers in May, some sterile and some fertile, like a lacecap hydrangea, poised horizontal on the tiered and spreading branches. The fact that its pendant leaves colour a sombre purple in the autumn, while its flowers turn to scarlet berries, seems an appropriately regal bonus.

Fourth, there is the Venetian sumach, *Continus coggygria* 'Notcutt's Variety'. I am nervous of this sumptuous colour in the garden, but at the same time deeply drawn to it. The leaves, almost as round and simple as tiddlywinks but a good deal bigger, are deepest plum colour; the plant works as a shadow even in the midday sun; its daintily self-coloured inflorescences are like skeletal flower sprays. In autumn its colour does not exactly change, but seems to grow transparent. It makes an exciting background to a flower arrangement if you put its stems in boiling water first, and it does not in the least mind being cut. In our garden, it is a background to rodgersias, by the pond.

Now for the late summer flowering shrubs that lured us. There is *Romneya coulteri*, the Californian tree poppy, alluring indeed, with those huge, white, papery, yellow-centred flowers that remind people of fried eggs; its stems and leaves are the grey-green of eucalyptus, and it sprawls about in the dry, warm earth under the sunbaked west wall of our cottage; it is said to be tender, that is why it is not more often seen; so far, for us, it has survived all winters; I treat it more like a herbaceous plant than a shrub, cutting it hard back in spring, for its top growth usually dies; but there are always new bits waiting to sprout, new stems running along the bricks at the base of our plaster wall. It starts to flower in July, and continues through August and September, with sometimes a stray flower or two in October and November. It is one of those gratifying plants which makes visitors to the garden exclaim with pleasure.

Then there is the 'Mount Etna' broom, *Genista aetnensis*, more of a tree now than a shrub, for it is as tall as the young cedar it stands beside. We made the classic amateur mistake and planted much too close; our imaginations failed to supply the dimensions of the future. Besides, we had been told that the broom is a short-lived beauty, and we reasoned that before the cedar had grown much, 'Mount Etna' would be dead. Now it rains its light, twiggy, almost leafless growth over the cedar's surface and shares its light, and the cedar has had to adjust its spreading branches. But we cannot wish death on our broom; it does not flower for long, but for two or three weeks of July it is a spectacular shower of gold.

Next comes its shorter and more generous relation, *Spartium junceum*, the Spanish broom, more generous because it flowers all summer long. Its pea flowers are larger and more isolated than 'Mount Etna's', and the bush itself shorter and less shapely; in fact, it is a half-wild, untidy thing. In spring-time, its shoots are often dead at the tips, for it inhabits a draughty corner near the house; I cut it back with secateurs, which takes ages for its stems seem endless, and it sends forth new green growths, the bearers of endless battalions of new, bright golden flowers.

With shrubs as with herbaceous plants, yellow and gold flowers haunt July and August; I have two bushes of St John's wort, not any old ones, but the fine *Hypericum* 'Hidcote', and nothing could be more golden than their cup-like flowers: buttercups on a grand scale. Recently I discovered that they, too, should be strictly pruned in spring if they are to be covered with August flowers. I now clip my two shrubs all over with the shears, as if they were lavender bushes, or dwarf hedges, and they respond with up to three feet of vigorous new growth.

Indeed, I suspect that all late summer flowering shrubs are better cut back in the spring; the beautiful *Hydrangea paniculata* with its white cones of flowers does not bloom at all for me unless spring-pruned. Similarly, I had years of sullen silence from two small and weedy *Hibiscus syriacus*, shrubby mallows, until I boldly cut them back one spring, to be rewarded, in August, with their hollyhock flowers which are *not* gold, but refreshingly pastel-coloured: 'Coeleste' is bluebell blue, splashed with maroon, and 'Hamabo' is white, splashed with pink. Now they have been joined by a specimen of the entrancing 'Blue Bird', whose late-summer freshness beckoned from a garden centre one day. I also cut back now a rarer shrub, the clerodendron or 'glory tree', a tall shrub with shapely leaves and subtle sprays of green and cream flowers in late summer followed by porcelain blue autumn berries. And I prune my little grey leaved caryopteris, to assure myself of its deep blue flower spikes in September.

I have never failed to prune my buddleias in spring and these are, in the end, my most valued August shrubs, because they bring the butterflies. I have a white one and a purple one, growing in rough grass in the field, but by far my most important buddleia, the one that really matters to me, is 'Lochinch'. I cut it back each year in April, to within an inch or two of last year's growth, and it rapidly grows out again, not into the usual gawky buddleia shape, but into a rounded, solid, many-branching shrub, each branch ending in long, tapering racemes of pale lavender, heavily scented flowers. I grow it in the herb garden, near the lavender hedges and the pots of blue agapanthus, and the lavender blue clematis 'Perle d'Azur' hangs over it, but all this mist and rain of lavender is offset by clouds of tortoiseshells, red admirals and peacock butterflies that hover over it whenever the sun shines. The peacocks, fluttering in the air, are points of blackness, because of the dark undersides of their wings; but as they come to rest upon the flowers, their spreading wings are the richest tawny venetian velvet with an azure eye in the corner. I purposely never eradicate all the nettles from the ditches, because without nettles for their eggs to rest on, there would be no peacock butterflies.

Summer passes, and the garden sinks into a semi-deadness: the flowering shrubs are over. Yellow leaves we have in plenty; we have, too, the toasted warmth of russet beech leaves. But what we want is red, and we have begun to get it. We now have a *Viburnum opulus* 'Notcutt's Variety', with vine-shaped leaves that colour scarlet, and with large, brilliant berries so clear and shiny they could be made of coloured glass all ready for a lady's necklace. Yet it is not exactly a sophisticated thing; its ancestors grow wild in the hedges as guelder roses, so it looks at home growing almost in the ditch that separates garden from wood, and it enjoys the moisture there. Then we have another *Cotinus coggygria*, the smoke bush, planted not far away from the purple-leafed one; its leaves are the same lovely round shape, but their colour, in October, is positively a blend of glowing sunset apricot and pink.

To carry the flag of autumn into the dull wood itself (for willow and elder and ash have little to give at this season) we have planted a spindle, *Euonymus* 'Red Cascade', where its red leaves and amazing pink-red fruits, splitting open as if they were the sepals of crystallised flowers, can be enjoyed at close quarters as we walk along the path. I plan to plant more spindles, so that they will fertilise each other and illuminate the wood with leaves and berries in late October.

So far, we have only two winter-flowering shrubs, but they are winners: *Hamamelis mollis* and *Viburnum fragrans*. Everybody knows the hamamelis ('Witch Hazel'); its twisty, globular, spidery yellow flowers are so remarkable, perched almost like exotic insects on its woody brown branches, each flower with a tiny dollop of wine-coloured velvet at its base; it is delicious in a winter vase; and the longer and more closely one studies its flowers, the more fascinated one becomes. However, it is slow of growth, and does not especially respond to being cut so, if one can afford it, one should plant two *Hamamelis mollis*. Because it is slow growing it is expensive; its leaves have a rather lifeless dullness so that it adds little to the summer scene, though it takes a pleasant, open, twisted shape, a little like magnolia, or like a little spreading tree painted on Christmas porcelain.

The winter-flowering viburnum we grow is a particularly good variety: *V.* × *bodnantense* 'Deben'; it is, on balance, the best winter-flowering shrub I know. Its white-pink, scented flowers really show up in the winter garden; unlike most winter shrubs, it has carrying quality; you can admire it from sixty yards away, and it blooms for a generous length of time; starting in November it is still performing four months later. Our five-year-old shrub is eight feet high; its scent is heady and its leaves turn red in autumn; the only thing it doesn't like is hard frost or snow, which turns its flowers brown; but if I had a gold medal to give out, I'd give it to this viburnum.

That completes our catalogue of flowering shrubs for high summer, autumn, winter. We have no rhododendrons, no azaleas – they'd look amiss in this neutral soil. Our only evergreen shrubs are hollies, five of them, planted between the cherry trees as a dark foil to the white blossom (an idea taken from Russell Page's *Education of a Gardener*). Hollies dislike being moved and are slow to restart growing, but when they do, they pick up speed and after many years ours are suddenly beginning to look like trees. It is satisfactory to have one's own holly to pick at Christmas time, but what I enjoy most about these hollies is the way their leaves glint like mirrors in the winter sun. Ours are self-fertile and free berrying, dark green with few prickles: *Ilex aquifolium* 'Pyramidalis', with slender, tapering growth to match their name.

In the end, my favourite shrubs are roses, the large, old-fashioned, trouble-free shrub roses that are so fashionable again as a corrective to the brilliant fire of floribundas flaming all summer long in orange, scarlet, copper, lemon, white, mauve, pink and crimson up and down the land. Their variety, their floriferousness, their months of bloom, their comparative cheapness, makes the floribundas hard to resist. It is particularly important, though difficult, to be strong-minded about them, and resist the temptation to have one of this and one of that, for the colours are clear, distinct notes, and do not seem to make harmonious chords when assembled together. But the main trouble with floribundas is that they lack grace; they seldom make shapely bushes, nor do they hold whatever shape they achieve since each year they must be quite severely pruned in order to throw out strong, angular growths anew. In the winter those growths are not a pleasing sight; they simply look as if they are waiting to be pruned, often with old leaves dangling; in the spring, cut down into short, stiff starfish by the secateurs, they are not pretty either. In summer, they ornament a garden and provide a succession of excellent, if lightly-scented, roses for the house; in short, the flowers are better than the plants they grow on.

With the old roses, the shrub roses, it is tempting to argue that the whole plant is more important than its individual flowers. But this would not be strictly true, for the most important thing about shrub roses is their profusion of flowers when they are in bloom. They cascade; they bloom all along the branches; and the branches themselves are wands, arching gracefully under the weight of flowers. The characteristic old rose forms a large shrub; it is a thing of shape and substance; it has pretty, healthy foliage and carries, in midsummer, hundreds of scented flowers in white or shades of blush or pink or violet. But it tends to be a less long-lasting cut-flower than a floribunda; its multitudinous petals are more fragile and delicate; its individual flowers are perhaps more muddled and, of course, it typically has only one flowering season: a few enchanted weeks in late June or in July.

For this reason, and because I hoped for late summer blooms, I planted Bourbon roses with their obliging, repeat-flowering habit; not only the two 'Zéphirine Drouhin's' by the door, but their pale sport, 'Kathleen Harrop', thornless and sweetly scented like the parent, and of a demure pink which escapes the possible vulgarity of 'Zéphirine', but at the same time seems to be denied her seductive charm. More exciting, I planted 'Mme Isaac Pereire', simply on the strength of descriptions in catalogues and books: 'Huge, double, richly scented . . . very large blooms with intense fragrance . . . a sumptuous beauty with a gorgeous scent.' She emerged from the printed page as a sort of miracle, perhaps the most heavenly-scented rose there is, variously described as 'richly-coloured', 'carmine', 'magenta', 'deep rose', 'crimson with purplish shading . . .' And she was praised for her second flowering, her blooms being said to achieve their greatest intensity in September. I cannot imagine anything more intense than the flowers my shrub produces in June/July. The word 'rich' recurs in all descriptions of her; she is richly perfumed, richly coloured; she is rich in the profusion of her flowering; rich in the multitude of velvet textured petals on each globed flower. A few flowers, picked when the dew has left them, yield scores of curving petals, gold-tipped where they meet the central stamens, for pot pourri. Long after they are dried, they retain a deep colour: pink-plum velvet. There seems no point in using any other rose for pot pourri, if this one is at hand.

The choosing of old roses from the wealth of albas, centifolias, damasks, chinas, mosses and gallicas is a heady and capricious affair, and everyone who grows them is likely to become emotional and partisan about the varieties they have chosen. Perhaps that is why written descriptions are often so persuasive: they are like love poems. But one man's love is not another's and here, as everywhere, one should try to see before one buys. The trouble is, the cut flowers will tell one little, thrust into a painted green metal vase at a flower show; one must see the whole shrub blooming, and it may be years before one can meet all these romantically named French and German ladies and gentlemen, cardinals, nymphs, angels and memories face to face. And meanwhile one is hasty to get going, to plant; I decided I must have a really parma violet rose, a rose that would show 'Mme Isaac Pereire' to be decidedly pink after all, so I looked at beautiful coloured photographs of old roses in a book, swithered between two gallicas: 'Cardinal Richelieu' and 'Charles de Mills', and chose the one that looked prettiest in the photograph: 'Charles de Mills'. It is a touchingly old-fashioned, muddle-centred rose with enough pink in its purple to remind one of the colour of blackberry juice mixed in milk, neat and tight-packed despite the complexity of its petal arrangement, and flat-faced, as if a knife had sliced across a globular rose at its equator. Its scent is exquisite, like its colour. Its stems have so many fine little green prickles on them that it can hardly be said to be thorny at all – more furry. Each year it grows fuller and rounder, stuck unceremoniously behind an apple tree; it is twiggy without being stiff and manages beautifully whether it is pruned or not.

Equally obliging, equally touching in its beauty, and even more cramped behind an apple tree, is the alba rose 'Céleste' – a superb, healthy plant. It is difficult to say whether its absolutely fresh, disease-free blue-green leaves, or its clusters of pale pink pointed buds is its strength, for its charm lies in its combination of leaf and flower. I grow this rose because a favourite aunt loved it and I knew it in her garden – sentimental reasons are as good as any for choosing amongst these roses.

I grow 'Constance Spry' because I fell in love with it myself when great branches of it were first displayed at a Royal Horticultural Society show in Vincent Square. Its cup-shaped flowers are unbelievably enormous, as many-petalled and voluptuous as 'Mme Isaac Pereire's', but its colour is infinitely more discreet, a ravishing pink which is pale at the edges and deeper in the folds and creases at the heart of the rose. It smells of an essence – perhaps vanilla, though an unsentimental friend identifies the scent of face-cream; one of its parents was a floribunda (which means it seems to demand pruning and, alas, is subject to black spot); but in spirit it is a centifolia; it is perhaps the most famous of David Austin's new race of 'English Roses', and is worthy to bear Constance Spry's name.

Then I grow a sweet rose I admired in full bloom in a Norfolk nursery at the end of August: 'Stanwell Perpetual', the *spinosissima* hybrid; its pale, blush-white flowers are modest but they sit prettily, either singly or in clusters, on the graceful branches it flings out in summer, embracing the sides of an Irish yew. Its leaves are small too, fern-like; its main flowering season proves to be June, and to call it 'perpetual' is optimistic, but it does repeat itself with single blossoms throughout the season.

The delightful fact about all these roses is that they mix beautifully together and are, indeed, loveliest mixed; at least the rule about planting several of a kind can be relaxed, or re-interpreted, here; several old roses together are indeed better than one isolated specimen, but each plant can be a different variety, and the subtly shaded palette, from blush-pink to purple, seems nothing but a series of variations on a single theme, a theme that has no trace of yellow in it.

And yet there are some almost indispensable yellow shrub roses; they are not categorised as 'Old Roses' in the catalogues, but rather as 'Species Roses' or 'Modern Specimens'. One of these I was again seduced into growing by the power of the printed word, in a book by Constance Spry herself. It is 'Frühlingsgold', another *spinosissima* hybrid, with large, almost single, creamy yellow flowers in late May on tall, arching stems; my aim is to surround its feet with purple flag irises, which bloom at the same time.

Then there is 'Canary Bird' – smaller, brighter flowers, well-named for their lyrical gaiety – tiny, May-flowering roses in profusion, tiny soft leaves, but huge bushes. I have already praised it in the chapter about hedges. I have also mentioned the pale pink hybrid musk roses that grow at each end of our pond; the flowers are not special, but the performance is, and the perpetual flowering habit and the musk scent that hangs on the air make them treasures. Stronger, coarser and more remarkable are the chalk white rugosa roses, also growing near the pond; one is *Rosa rugosa alba*, whose hips are sealing-wax red, like small tomatoes. The other is the first shrub rose that ever caught my eye: the celebrated rugosa, 'Blanc Double de Coubert', which I saw growing as an isolated specimen in the grass at Kew Gardens, its bright green, crinkled leaves half hidden by frilly tissue-paper flowers like double white camellias. I think rugosas, with their iron constitutions, liberal repeat-flowering, utter resistance to disease and true rose scent would be the easiest of all roses to grow were it not that, strong as they are, they are inclined to sucker.

There are four more roses to be listed: the first is 'Frühlings-morgen', pretty cousin to 'Frühlingsgold': it is perfectly named, its single flowers are the pink, white and gold of some imagined dawn in spring; it is like the sweet briar of English hedges five times magnified in size, growing on a tall and upright shrub. The second is the species *Rosa moyesii*, taller still, nine or ten feet high, a noble shrub, slender and graceful, with delicate leaves and small, single, warm red, almost tawny flowers. People whom I admire, admire this rose, and I partly grow it for their sakes. It has a wildling air about it, untamed, not rich and perfumed as I like a rose to be, but faintly exotic like a flower on a Persian embroidery, and its colour does not quite mix with the cool pinks of the old French roses, and perhaps it should not grow near them. Its hips are exotic too: slender, bottle-shaped, warm orange. Third comes the much-acclaimed modern shrub rose 'Nevada', which holds its wide open ivory flowers with such panache all along its branches in its first flush of June flowering, and then gives a brief encore in August, when it sometimes surprises us with pale pink buds. Finally there is a rose widely admired and recommended now: *Rosa rubrifolia*, the red-leafed rose, grown for its foliage and hips alone. Its flowers are small, single, pink, white-centred, of fleeting significance compared with the bloom of its leaves. It is not quite right to describe those leaves as red, for they are also blue –

wine-coloured with a grey-blue bloom over the surface, as if a glaucous mist had condensed on them; the hips come in abundant clusters, glossy as conkers but brilliant red. The bush has a lovely shape; it is one of the roses with gracefully arching wands; and it seeds itself, so there is the thrill of finding a new little rubrifolia growing in some quite humble and unexpected place.

Almost all these roses came as comparatively late additions to our garden. Most grow on either side of the old gravel path that leads from the front door to the shed. For some years, I thought it too obvious to put borders down this path: too obvious, and too much work. But as one part of a garden establishes and grows tame, one longs to start another, and I told myself, quite rightly, that shrub roses are not much trouble and combine happily in spirit with apple trees. So now the species roses, tall, single-flowered and free-standing, grow on the right of the path, with flag irises, Canterbury bells, self-seeding valerian and sweet rocket at their feet and the persian lilacs in between them; the showy old roses grow on the left, trained against a wire-netting fence which was originally erected in the hope of confining two bumptious young dogs within a restricted area of the garden. That hope proved futile, but the fence remained as a prop for the roses which were in the first place designed to mask it. Old roses are easy to train against a fence like this – much easier, because less vigorous, than real climbers; you simply pull some of their strong canes into a near-horizontal position and attach them to the netting with a green garden twist or bit of string; then they send up flowering shoots all the way along the horizontal stems. Each plant must occupy at least nine feet of fence; 'Celestial' meets 'Constance Spry', whose pale pink blooms touch 'Mme Isaac Pereire's' in early July; 'Mme Isaac Pereire' mingles in turn with the pale pink of 'Kathleen Harrop', and beyond is 'Charles de Mills' whose purple stretches out to meet the little white 'Stanwell Perpetual'. When they are all out, at midsummer, the sight is so joyous, the scent so abundant, that one can only laugh and say: 'Look at the roses!' Or perhaps someones says: 'The roses are specially good this year.' But they have forgotten: the roses are good every year.

Instead of being satisfied, I wanted more. Perhaps everybody who grows roses wants more. I dreamt of a rose garden proper. It was partly the name 'rose garden' that tempted me, and I knew where it should be. It should be at the far end of the herbaceous border, through the arch in the hornbeam hedge where an enclosed space waited to be filled. There should be a curving path through it leading gently to the pond. I drew it many times on paper, each time differently; sometimes it was like a formal parterre, with clipped edgings; sometimes it flowed in curves; sometimes, on summer afternoons when no-one was there to say: 'What are you doing? We've got too much garden already,' I furtively but oh, so pleasurably, busied myself with bamboo canes, sticking them into the ground at the proposed corners of the beds, and snaked the garden hose round their hypothetical contours. Sometimes the paths were grassy, sometimes paved. Sometimes there was an imaginary sundial at a central point; sometimes, even, another lily pond.

Now I have made it. The space is long and asymmetric, with hornbeam hedges on two sides and the 'Canary Bird' hedge and donkey shed on a third. There are three simple beds with curved fronts and straight backs, rather like attenuated capital 'D's. They are arranged end to end from north to south, the straight sides parallel with the hornbeam hedge; they are surrounded with grass. Each has a weeping standard rose 'Albéric Barbier' in the middle. Viewed from one end of the rose garden, the standards should be exactly in line. Round the curved front of each bed is a thick edging of *Alchemilla mollis*, which has to be renewed with fresh seedlings every third year to stop it encroaching seriously upon the roses. Along the back of each bed is catmint. In the corners we plan clipped box globes; as each bed has two corners there will be a line of six box globes one day. I think such rhythmic patterns are part of what 'rose garden' suggests.

The making of the garden spread over three years – a bed a year. There is a comparatively easy way of making new beds in grass; you peg out the boundaries with bamboos and string; you then water all over the grassy surface of the future bed with paraquat, then, to hide the ugly yellowing grass, you cover it with hedge clippings or any other handy mulch. In a few weeks' time, the grass is dead. You can begin to trench the bed without the bother of lifting and transporting turves. I dug and trenched the first bed in a hot August. The earth was in dry clods full of ant holes which held their shapes when spaded. Each clod had to be cut and cut with a spade to break it up after turning. Into the trenches went six barrowloads of promising brown compost. And into the bed that autumn went an assortment of shell pink roses.

A year later, I dug the second bed. This time the summer was wet, the earth under the mulch of yew clippings was slimy and mossy. I dug up an apostle spoon and a George V penny, and put in a job lot of not very convincing compost. Into this second bed went creamy, buff and amber roses.

The third bed, duly materialising a year later, held white roses.

Pink, buff, amber and white: an unadventurous, not to say insipid colour scheme. To make up, there is an adventurous mixture of roses within the scheme: hybrid musks, hybrid perpetuals, polypompoms, hybrid teas and floribundas. The hybrid tea is Peter Beales' shell pink 'Anna Pavlova'. He describes it as the most heavily perfumed rose he knows; it is the most perfect, high-centred hybrid tea shape that I have ever seen. Alas – under my inexpert pruning, its growth is leggy. The pale pink floribunda growing with it is the heavily scented 'English Miss'; the white in the third bed is 'Iceberg'. The clusters of generous, continuous flowering floribunda roses show above the alchemilla edging all round the fronts of their respective beds; so I make my peace with this maligned but miraculous race. The polypompom, growing round the front of the middle bed, is short and bushy, an Edwardian bedding rose with big clusters of peachy-cream flowers, 'Grüss an Aachen' – a real winner in everything but scent. Behind it is the hybrid perpetual 'Lady Hillingdon', another tall rose even in its bush form, but leafy rather than leggy, with plum red stems and a hint of purple in the rich green leaves. The flowers above these sombre colours are a *tour de force*: slender pointed buds opening to loose petalled velvety flowers of incandescent apricot, with a scent to match.

The hybrid musk roses go along the backs of the three beds: two pink 'Felicia' in the first, two 'Buff Beauty' in the second, and two of the delicate white 'Moonlight' in the third, with its extra long clusters of single flowers.

Last autumn I bought a small wooden seat with a curved back in a local auction sale. I plan to put it in the corner of the rose garden this summer, and spend a lot of time sitting on it and looking at these roses.

XI

The Vegetable Garden

It started as eight raspberry canes planted in a trench somewhere in the middle of the field – a present from an aunt. The couch grass encroached on them and we decided to cultivate a larger patch round them and 'grow some veggies'. A neighbour came with a rotavator and soon a rectangle of brown, ploughed earth lay round the raspberries. This field had lain fallow for some years, but had once been cultivated by a neighbouring farmer, and the ploughed soil looked good. It was easy to dig, well drained, and a nice, warm brown colour, sloping slightly southwards – just the thing for the crop we had set our sights on: asparagus. We would make an asparagus bed, now, so that we should have the maximum number of greedy years ahead in which to enjoy it.

We ordered seventy-five plants. We did not prepare the ground very well – we were still too busy doing other things; we did not build up the beds; we simply ploughed in some cow manure with the borrowed rotavator. The plants arrived; it was at Easter, rather cold and raining gently. The book said that asparagus crowns must not be kept waiting a moment more than was necessary. I worked doggedly along in the wet trench, pressing each crown onto a hastily fashioned little mound, then spreading the pale, spidery roots down the sides of the mound according to the book. As I worked my heart was in my sodden gumboots for I saw little broken pieces of couch grass left by the rotavator in the soil all the way along. This seemed typical of our gardening: too much haste and optimism, nothing thorough, skilled or careful; seventy-five expensive two-year-old asparagus plants stuck into couch-infested ground. Still, the asparagus came up temptingly; I hand-weeded round it, very carefully, with a narrow, pointed trowel, and we did not cut it; it

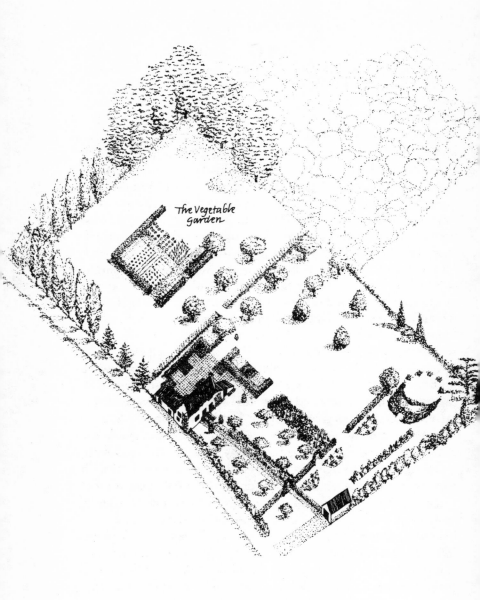

The vegetable garden and rose beds.

turned to pretty fern, two feet high. In December I cut the stems at ground level and mulched the beds with cow manure. The next year we again resisted eating it, weeded the beds again, cut down and mulched again in winter. In the third year after planting, we began to cut and eat. We have harvested increasingly large crops of asparagus ever since, cutting, at ground level, every succulent green and purple tip that showed its head between April and mid-June. We can never miss a weekend during that season, for if the shoots are not cut, they turn quickly to fern. On arrival at the cottage, in the twilight, we rush to the asparagus bed, and exclaim in a mixture of delight and dismay at how toweringly tall some of the shoots have grown and how urgent a matter it is to eat them. Fresh asparagus from the garden is different in kind from bunches of bought asparagus, tightly tied with raffia in the greengrocer's shop; it turns brilliant green when it is cooked and cooks quickly, and is so tender that you can eat its stem right down to the very end. It seems that, if asparagus really likes its site (which means that it is well-drained), then it will prove itself stronger than couch grass, and the whole mystique of the beautifully built-up and rounded asparagus bed will be unnecessary. One need only cut down and mulch in winter, and weed by running a gloved hand over the beds and combing or massaging the surface with spread fingers in the spring. In wet summers, the weeding continues, despite the fact that nowadays we water the surface of the beds with weed killer before the first shoots appear. Sometimes a kind friend who asks to help in the garden can be put to weed a yard or two of the asparagus bed. By August, the forest of fern is so thick as to bar all entry, so the weeding can cease. It is a beautiful, as well as a delicious, crop; the tall, strong ferns adorn our vegetable garden, almost dividing it in two during the summer, for the two beds run across the middle of the patch from side to side. In the autumn the plants turn gold, with red berries on the females (whose strength, unfortunately, goes into seeding themselves prodigiously). In fact, they supply some of the warmest autumn colour in the garden. But I must end on a less self-congratulatory note, and remember the poplar suckers that are now appearing in the beds, having travelled over half a field to share this delicious soil. And the moles have arrived, too.

Near the asparagus, we planted rhubarb, four roots given us by a neighbour. These roots have prospered to the extent that they threaten to dominate the kitchen garden; they produce stems like tree-trunks, and the occasional soaring green flower (much disapproved of by serious rhubarb-fanciers, though esteemed by flower-arrangers). By May their huge, umbrella leaves get in the way of anything planted near, but provide excellent cool packing material for covering baskets of flowers or vegetables bound for a car ride to London. In the spring, we have persuaded ourselves that we enjoy rhubarb fool, if not rhubarb crumble.

Below the asparagus, and above the rhubarb, we began to grow our 'few veggies' – early potatoes, French beans, radishes. We followed a book, as all amateur vegetable growers must do; ours was a simple paperback, Brian Furner's *The Kitchen Garden*. I often had it open on the soil beside me as I drew my hoe along a drill, so as to get my spacings right; its pages are now dirty with earth. To our incredulous pleasure, the seeds germinated, the crops grew, bore fruit, were delicious. On winter evenings the seed catalogues by the fire made heady reading. We expanded our vegetable patch to accommodate more rows: peas, spinach, courgettes. Old, scribbled, out-of-date plans of how the planting should go, year after year, allowing for annual rotation of crops, lay round the kitchen. We wanted sweetcorn, tomatoes; we expanded the plot again, each spring borrowing our kindly neighbour's rotavator and ploughing in as much compost as we could. We decided to make the vegetable garden into more of an event by putting a hedge round it – really, we were so enamoured of hedges and the service they were doing to our windswept garden that we were always on the lookout for another place where we could plant one. We put beech round two sides and privet along a third (a curious choice, but we wanted quick, evergreen privacy to the east). The fourth side we left open, as a site for rubbish, compost and bonfire. When the hedges had grown, they made good horticultural sense, filtering winds that would otherwise have flattened vulnerable crops. Today the vegetable garden feels warm when you step into it; the hedges have turned it into a real kitchen garden, the next best thing to the walled garden we would dearly love to have possessed, with espaliered fruit trees against flint or brick. It now measures forty-five feet by fifty-four feet, and in theory it can still go on growing on its open, southern boundary.

It is easy to get into a rut with vegetables, as with cooking. One should resolve, each year, to try new things. Recently a few extra yards of ground taken in have made room for two double rows of broad beans. They are a promising sight in May — robust, succulent, blue-green, their chubby leaves arranged like rosettes all round the stems, the perfume from their white, ebony-blotched flowers hanging sweetly on the air to attract the bees. I am glad I followed the book's advice and planted in double rows: they look neat but lavish.

Neat but lavish — that is how the whole vegetable garden should look. There is infinite satisfaction to be had from just looking at a vegetable garden, if its rows are straight and parallel. Mine used to wobble, and stop half-way along to give way to something else. I know better now; with the help of garden twine pulled tight between sticks, and a certain amount of striding and pacing and lining-up between rows, and above all my husband's straight eye, we get our rows roughly right, and as the crops begin to grow in lines of contrasting greens they provide, ironically, one of the most pleasing sights in the whole garden.

It is ironic because the motive for growing vegetables is clearly not artistic; the motive is a potent mixture of the economic and the greedy. There are few things more gratifying than to bring a brimming colander of home-grown vegetables into the kitchen

and tell yourself, as your mouth begins to water over their freshness and plenty, that they have cost you nothing but a fraction of
the price of a seed packet. They have cost, in fact, many hours
of labour, but it is labour of the most instinctive and therapeutic
kind. I believe that now I spend more time with the vegetables
than with the flowers, because even when the sowing and
thinning and staking is done, there remains the weeding and
watering. The little weeds flourish in the newly turned soil; even
if they did not steal nourishment from the vegetables, the
dedicated vegetable gardener would still reach for his hoe
knowing that, if his rows are to look really nice, the soil must be
bare between them. Ours never is: it is weed-infested, with
variable areas of comparative neatness and always some
shameful corners which I intend to deal with later on. But I
understand that compulsive drive towards neatness that can
hold the vegetable gardener quietly enslaved with hoe, hand,
and trowel, a kneeling figure amongst his vegetables, for hours.

And then there is the picking. That, too, is time-taking
happiness, moving slowly along sun-warmed rows, your fingers
searching for cool peapods or sticky beans or ripening courgettes lurking secretly in the darkness under their large leaves
and golden trumpet flowers. Which leads me to list, in order of
sowing, the varieties of vegetables we harvest.

Shallots: this is the first crop to be planted in the spring, and
one of the easiest of all. We push the bulbs of 'Giant Yellow' into
the ground eight inches apart in March, until just their brown
papery points are showing. The birds inspect them, but do not
seem to like them. Quickly they make their green shoots above
ground and multiply their little brown-skinned bulbs beneath
it. In July they are ready to be lifted, dried, and sometimes
amateurishly plaited or braided into an imitation French onion
string to dangle from the rafters. They are smaller than onions
and gentler in flavour and suit some digestions better. Also they
are much harder to buy in the shops. They are lovely for
flavouring tomato or potato salad.

Garlic: this is an even easier crop than shallots; you simply split up one plump bulb of garlic into its individual cloves and plant these at the same distance apart as the shallots and at about the same time. The resultant shoots look tall and wispily single in comparison to the generously bunched shoots of the shallots, but it is highly satisfactory to harvest ten pieces of garlic for the price of one, and the growing plants are said to keep pests at bay. I have used garlic from the delicatessen for my initial source, but find garlic from a seed merchant is plumper and fresher.

Potatoes: we grow 'earlies', and experiment with different varieties: 'Sutton's Foremost', 'Homeguard', 'Pentland Javelin', 'Dunluce' (from Marshalls), 'Maris Bard' and 'Maris Peer'. Though we have particularly liked these last two, we suspect that the variety chosen is less important than the weather. We try to remember to order early, and when the plastic bucket of seed potatoes arrives we immediately unpack the tubers and balance them on end in shallow boxes, each propped against its neighbour with the end which has the most eyes pointing upwards. There they remain, indoors and in a good light, until they have sprouted. We plant, superstitiously, on Good Friday, whenever Easter may fall, following tradition, and start lifting in July. Potatoes, planted by someone with a straight eye, make a vegetable garden look orderly; the dark green leaves furnish it and when the plants are 'earthed up' (which is not strictly necessarily with 'earlies') the resultant parallel furrows look neater still. Digging up a few potatoes for dinner is one of the quickest, pleasantest forms of harvesting; there is always hopeful curiosity to see how many new potatoes the fork has turned up, lying pale and clean-looking on the dark soil; the number will, of course, depend largely on the rainfall; we have learnt, in a dry spring, to train the hose on the potatoes. We do not lift them, even when the foliage has died down, until we are ready to eat them. They seem to taste better, straight from the earth, and their skins rub off more quickly under the kitchen tap. Sometimes, in addition to our 'earlies', we get hold of the scarce potato 'Pink Fir Apple', cylindrical and knobbly, said to be the best there is for potato salad, with paper-thin skin and waxy flesh, tasting like a new potato even at Christmas time.

Broad Beans: these go in at roughly the same time as the potatoes. We have grown 'Masterpiece Green Longpod' and also the dwarf variety 'The Sutton', which may be useful in a small garden as the catalogue claims, and certainly needs no staking, but we would rather concentrate on taller plants with a promise of heavier cropping. It is not difficult to stake broad beans; you put a row of canes all along each side of the double row at regular intervals like fence posts, and then run one or two strings along from cane to cane, so that if the cropping plants begin to flop sideways, the strings sustain them. Nor is it difficult to control the dreaded blackfly, by pinching out all the succulent growing tips and spraying affected stems with a solution of washing-up liquid and water. If we find a grievously infested plant amongst healthy ones, we pull it out and put it on the bonfire.

Salsify (the oyster plant): this is a show-off vegetable, but not difficult to grow, though it occupies its site all spring and summer long, and is not lifted until the winter. It tastes good with melted butter but is not altogether different in taste from a parsnip, only thinner, more whiskered and corrugated, and much harder to scrub and peel.

Parsnips: these seem, on the whole, a better proposition than the gastronomically impressive salsify, so we have switched our allegiance to parsnip 'Tender and True'. We try to sow it in April and thin to six inches apart in June or July, but often the sowing does not get done till May. The following winter the parsnips really come into their own, hanging on even in frozen ground when all other crops are long since harvested.

Carrots: the same routine applies with carrots as with parsnips, except that we start thinning when they are an inch or so tall and have always eaten the lot before midwinter. It seems impossible to sow carrot seed thinly enough to save the initial thinnings; we have tried mixing the seed with sand but this only produced an unsatisfactory sequence of gaps and clumps along the row. We do, however, mix the seed with a combined seed dressing, shaking a little of this clinging white powder with the seeds in their packet before sowing, and scattering a further dressing along the drill as a protection against the carrot fly which always threatens to scar the crop with black rings and pock marks. When the major thinning takes place in July, the thinnings will be delicious young carrots ready for the pot, but the ferny tops must be buried deep in the compost heap, not impatiently broken off and discarded, attracting carrot fly by their smell. I like the tapered varieties best, like the very long 'New Red Intermediate', though we have often grown the snub-nosed, cylindrical varieties like 'Autumn Ring' or 'Nantes', and are influenced in our choice, not by experience, but by the photographs in seed catalogues.

Spinach: this works best when there is lots of rain and the ground is fairly rich; after all, its leaves are composed mainly of water. And even when it flourishes, it all too quickly runs to seed. But we love fresh spinach, so we persevere, and we have had good success two years running with a variety called 'Sigmaleaf' from Suttons, sowing in succession at various different dates from April until June. We have also tried the small-leafed spreader, New Zealand spinach, which is drought resistant, but 'shy to germinate' and not specially nice to eat. Our greatest success has been with 'Perpetual Spinach' or spinach beet. Once it has outgrown danger from slugs, and been sternly thinned to leave six-inch gaps between seedlings, it settles down to produce large leaves all summer long, without a sign of seeding during its first summer. Perhaps it is not quite as succulent as spinach proper, and its stems are coarser, but in flavour it is almost indistinguishable, it is quicker to prepare and it freezes well.

Turnips: these are the easiest possible vegetable to grow; the seed germinates like chickweed, and the only trouble is to thin the seedlings adequately if you want to eat the turnips. If, on the other hand, you sow turnip seed because you have heard it is a way of discouraging couch grass from the soil, you don't even have to thin it and you can dig the turnips into the soil again in winter.

Radishes: almost as easy as turnips, and gratifyingly quick to mature providing they get water in dry weather and are thinned enough for each little plant to have room in which to swell. We have usually grown 'French Breakfast' because of its appealing name, but we are tiring of its long, cylindrical shape and may try a round variety like Suttons 'Scarlet Globe' next year.

Lettuce: this is another crop for successional sowing. Again, there is an initial battle with slugs, but germination is so quick that in the end we usually have enough lettuces for the summer, filling the gaps made by early picking with seedlings from a later sowing. We look no further than the large, crisp 'Webb's Wonder'. Why not grow the lettuce which is always the most expensive in the shops?

Globe Artichokes: here, the variety is important. I grew some plants from seed years ago and, though they were robust and frighteningly perennial, the artichokes they produced were not true to type, but stiffly-needled as sea-urchins, so that it was dangerous to peel the petals, and barely worth it since the taste was mediocre. The best thing to do with these home-bred artichokes was to let them flower – the honey-scented, electric-blue, giant, domed flower-heads were a wonder, worth picking and studying at close quarters indoors, like the tufted crest of some paradise bird. But the desired globe artichokes for cooking have gently tapered, juicy petals and delicious hearts, and do not grow into such formidable towers; nor are they so perennial. Indeed, one is advised to renew them from their offshoots every other year. The variety to go for is 'Gros Vert de Laon', or perhaps 'Green Globe'.

Green Peas: peas are a great deal of trouble, and a recurrent source of disappointment, but in a good year the reward is priceless. No greengrocer's shop and no frozen packet can equal the taste of young peas picked half-an-hour ago from the garden, so we persevere. We used to favour the French *petit pois*, 'Gullivert', but it took a long time to shell enough pods to make a dishful of *petit pois*, and the taste was not noticeably different from that of any young garden peas picked before the pods reach the drum-tight stage so, after trying various more conventional peas like 'Kelvedon Wonder', we have settled for the early maincrop variety, 'Hurst Green Shaft', with its double pods each containing as many as nine or twelve perfect peas. We also grow mangetout peas, selecting whatever variety the catalogues offer, though the choice is unfortunately becoming very thin. At present we grow 'Oregon Sugar Pod', which remains delicious even after the pods have swelled. Mangetouts are marvellous, economical things; in some seasons they bear, if you keep picking them, for about six weeks and they are the exact opposite of *petit pois*, for they are no work to prepare at all; you simply pinch off each end of the pod with your thumb-nail and finger and cook the lot. They are just as delicious served cold, with salad dressing, as hot.

We usually sow peas in early May because there has been no time in April. A week before sowing, we dress the soil with Growmore; then we plant very painstakingly in triple, staggered rows in a flat-bottomed trench. They look like the beginnings of a smocking pattern, diamond-shaped diagonals laid out on the ground. For pea-sticks, I save bits of hazel, elder and willow from the previous summer's hedge prunings, and bamboo cut from a large clump by the pond. It is a laborious business, collecting enough stakes of suitable length and erecting them along each side of every row, slanting slightly inwards like a rudimentary wig-wam. I then embark on an even more time-consuming project, weaving black nylon thread to and fro, up and down, from side to side between the stakes, following Brian Furner's patent technique for supporting the pea tendrils and keeping off the birds at one and the same time. The weeding, then, is endless, a matter of hands and knees along the rows, plucking baby nettles and thistles, grass and groundsel, chickweed and fat hen from amongst the seedlings, and doing one's best not to pull out pea plants by mistake. I do not know why in some years germination seems so partial. I believe that many creatures – mice? slugs? pigeons? – agree with us that peas have the loveliest taste of all, and beat us to them at very early stages in the growing cycle, sometimes even before they have broken through the earth. Then, in a good year, the vines grow thick and tall; my staking proves inadequate and the crops end by breaking over and bowing forward in tangled chaos. But the clusters of peas still live and dangle beneath the mess, and I always mulch between the rows with straw or cut grass to suppress the weeds and keep the broken pea-vines clean. The mulch also helps to keep moisture in. Peas can look miserable in a dry summer, and need to be well watered when the white flowers appear.

French Beans: we grow dwarf French beans, sometimes one variety, sometimes another, usually green, occasionally purple (changing to green in boiling water). But whether they are called 'Tendergreen' or 'Masterpiece', 'The Prince' or 'Royalty' they are unfailingly delicious. The yield from one quarter pint packet gives us continuous large helpings for about six weeks, or many polythene bags filled for the freezer. It is a mistake to sow too early, safest to delay till the very end of May or early June. Often there will be bare stretches in the initial rows, where further marauders have eaten the heart out from the seed before it breaks the surface of the soil, but the seed packets are always so generous that almost indefinite reinforcements can be sown, and in the end perseverance is rewarded and one can achieve two long, full rows. Indeed, it is a good idea to stagger sowings: there will be tender beans for longer. I plant the sleek brown seeds crossways eight inches apart along the two-inch deep trench, and when the plants are a few inches high I push twigs in between them, to stop them from keeling over later on and, as with peas, mulch between the rows with compost, straw or grass cuttings. French beans are less of a nuisance than peas, less affected by drought, last longer and are, indeed, our Number One Success.

We do not bother with scarlet runners, which must surely be more trouble to train and support and are certainly more trouble to prepare for the pot, since they need to be sliced, not merely topped and tailed like French beans; they come later, too, when the holidays are half over, and in my opinion are decidedly less delicious (disintegrating in their tiresome little oblique slices before they leave the boiling water) than the beautifully whole, firm French bean. Of course they are beautiful climbers in their own right with their scarlet flowers, and must be a boon where space is short.

Courgettes: here again, it does not seem to matter which variety one grows, providing the seeds are listed as courgettes and not as marrows; whether they are labelled 'Zucchini' or 'Green Bush F1 Hybrid' they have always proved good, so far. Lacking a cold frame, we sow our seeds under jam jars at the end of May, pushing two seeds into the earth under each jar at the spot where they are to grow, so that we end up with a row of about eight jam jars three feet apart. About a fortnight later there are usually two strong seedlings spreading their first pair of oval leaves under each jar; the weaker must sadly be discarded, along with the jar itself, though they sometimes agree to transplant. Provided the seeds have been set in a reasonably fertile spot (the site of an old rubbish heap is excellent) and they can be watered in dry weather, there is nothing more to do about them but wait for the series of golden trumpet flowers to come and with them the baby marrows. As fast as you pick them, more will come and if, occasionally, you miss one lurking beneath the leaves, it is pleasant to have a fresh, full-grown marrow for a change. I have not found that the odd marrow puts an end to the production of courgettes, as the experts warn.

Tomatoes: tomatoes go so well with courgettes in cookery that they come next to mind. Again, lacking a green-house, I buy about eight tomato plants in May or early June, and am always surprised by their comparative cheapness. In a warm summer one is picking ripening tomatoes by late August; in a dull summer, there are masses of beautiful pale green tomatoes for chutney. I am weary of the ubiquitous variety called 'Money-maker', perhaps because of the self-advertising name, and have had small success with the increasingly popular 'Alicante'. I plump enthusiastically for the prolific and tasty 'Ailsa Craig' and for the early, generous 'Outdoor Girl', though we have also grown 'Holland Hybrid', 'Shirley', and the two bush varieties: 'Marmande' with large, thin-skinned, asymmetric fruits, and 'Sleaford Abundance'. Eight plants do not take up much room, and all you need are eight tall stakes, a handful of twists, manure or compost for a mulch, a bottle of patent tomato fertiliser for a weekly feed once the fruitlets have formed, and lots of water in dry weather. I fill each hole with at least one can of water before setting out the plants. Pinching out the little growths that sprout from the leaf axils, and the wayward growths that sometimes come curling from the base of the plant, is important, but easy, and puts the warm, lingering, peppery smell of tomato foliage on your fingers. Sometimes the leaves of a tomato plant will turn suspiciously crackly and dry as harvest time approaches; I pull the worst leaves off the plant and hope for the best. At other times, yellow blotches will appear on leaves, or hard brown blotches on the fruit. I have studied depressing horticultural articles about tomato fungus diseases like stem rot and blight but have failed to make a convincing diagnosis, so if the blotches are bad I dig the whole plant up and put it on the bonfire. We always plant in a different place each year.

Sweet Corn: only swift-sowing varieties are possible for us, since we need something that can be sown in the open when danger of frosts is past, and it has to be extremely quick if we are to have corn before the frosts start again. Fortunately we have discovered that corn is very sweet before it is officially ripe; the pale young heads beneath the blanched cream silk and the tissue-paper wrapping leaves can be bitten right through and eaten like asparagus. They are more delicate than the ripe gold cobs on the uneatable fibrous cores which emerge when the silk turns brown and dry – the official sign that the corn is ready for eating. Our usual variety is called 'First of All' and we plant it in block formation: five plants by five plants either way in a square, to encourage germination. This takes some contriving in a garden where most other crops are arranged in lines, which is why our sweet corn sometimes finishes beside the garden pond, where its rushy leaves look well.

Flowers: inspired by views of bright and neat Dutch and French kitchen gardens, glimpsed from train windows on continental holidays, where vegetables mingle with annual flowers, I have taken to sowing sunflowers along the path that bisects our patch, and sweet peas on the other side. The sunflowers are 'Giant Yellow' – seven-foot wonders with huge round cheerful faces drooping modestly at the top of their arching necks; the sweet peas are sometimes 'Antique Fantasy' with small flowers in deep red, white, purple and pink, and sometimes 'Painted Lady', white with red edges, both old-fashioned varieties offered by Thompson and Morgan on the grounds of their surpassingly sweet scent. But I find the flowers fade disappointingly fast in water, and the divine scent fades quickly too, and I am no longer convinced that they are more desirable than modern Spencer varieties. The principle of mixing rows of flowers with the vegetables remains an appealing one; I plan to find a home for exiled hybrid tea and floribunda roses at the edge of the vegetable garden one day. No doubt 'flowers for picking' used always to be a feature of walled kitchen gardens in Edwardian England, but the practice has disappeared along with the kitchens.

Soft Fruits: here there is mainly failure to report; our gooseberry bushes are all twig and leaf, no berries; either the birds take all the fruit or else I do not prune the bushes properly, for all the hours I spend in early spring anxiously cutting amongst the piercing thorns. I do not know why it is that, however much I study the helpful diagrams of 'how to prune' in fruit-growing manuals – the photographs showing before-and-after views of the same bush, with dotted transverse lines labelled 'cut here' – as soon as I get outdoors with my secateurs and face my own complexity of branch and twig, I am uncertain where to cut. My bushes bear no relation to the photographed bushes in books. I could give a lecture on the principles of pruning, but I cannot put the principles into practice. We have not tried our hand at redcurrants and blackcurrants; as for those eight raspberry canes which started our vegetable garden off – they fell victim to virus disease some years ago.

The vegetable garden is thus a blend of success and failure; one should, in theory, follow up the successes and reject the things that fail. But the very essence of vegetable gardening is renewal, a cycle of hope, disappointment, fulfilment, and hope again.

XII

The View

The garden goes on growing. It looks different today from how it looked when I sat down to write Chapter I. Some things have died; some things have sickened; some corners which were airy and fertile now seem dank and overgrown; the farmer who used to let me have farmyard manure has moved away, and with him the dairy herd on the meadows. One apple, 'Ellison's Orange', and one pear, 'Beurre Superfin', have succumbed to canker and been axed. All the flag irises are browning at the tips. Black aphids seem to burn the growing points of the ornamental cherries. Families of vivid caterpillars are feeding on the beech leaves. Worst of all, the glorious lilies, madonnas, tigers, *L. henryi*, are all stricken with botrytis. To brood and worry, to search out signs of pests and plant sickness, seems an inescapable part of the gardening condition. Pessimistic moods, like caterpillars, feed on the gardener's happiness.

Then hope returns, or one would not be a gardener. I have drenched the soil round the lilies with systemic fungicide, and I shall spray the young growths with copper in the spring. I have bought a long wand called a 'tumbleweeder', a splendidly efficient little glyphosate atomiser, and a pot of glyphosate gel. I plan to do battle on the weeds once more, armed with wand and spray. I shall use the little brush supplied in the pot of gel and paint the most offending bindweed leaves with individual strokes. Perhaps, after years of defeat, victory is at hand.

The gardener is also beset by restlessness. No sooner is one part of the garden tamed, than another presents itself for treatment. In this way, over twenty years, our herb garden doubled in size, our peach garden was formed, our pond was dug, to say nothing of our ditch garden, our subsidiary yew hedge was planted, our rose garden was realised, and we started

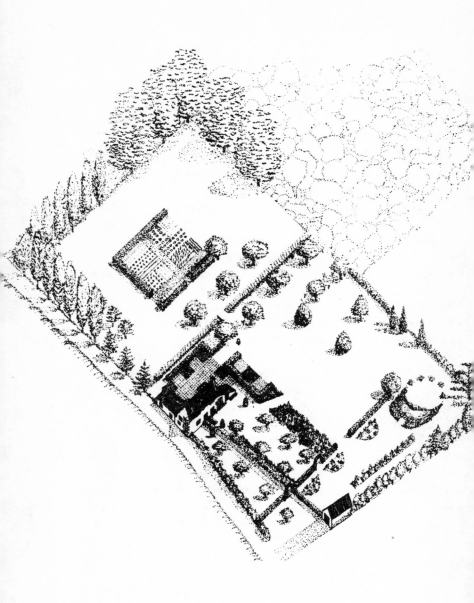

The garden after 20 years.

planting in the wood. And that was not enough: I made a second herbaceous border.

The narrow bed in which the old roses were planted had become a little wider every year to make room for all manner of herbaceous plants overflowing from the main herbaceous border or expelled from it. Clumps of Japanese anemones, *Achillea* 'Gold Plate', sibirican irises and veronica moved in first; then *Salvia superba*, *Sedum spectabile* 'Autumn Joy', *Chrysanthemum maximum* and *Alchemilla mollis*. Dwarf shrubs came too, moved from earlier, unsatisfactory places; the late summer-flowering caryopteris, low and silver-leaved with deepest violet-blue flowers, and the gentle herbaceous clematis, *Clematis davidiana*, with pretty vine-like leaves and little washed-out blue flowers. Finally came clumps of border phlox in pink and white from a neighbour's garden. I was within an ace of having twin borders, nodding to each other across the grass. (See Plate 2.)

It was a chance to grow grander herbaceous flowers, those archetypal flowers of country calendars. So peonies came, a collection of half-a-dozen scented varieties, for how can you have a cottage garden without peonies? I wanted to see their red, bent-over shoots elbowing through the soil in spring. Lupins came, sown from seed, in lovely colours of pink and primrose and dusky plum. Best of all, delphiniums came, three noble survivors from one of Blackmore and Langdon's seedling offers, with towering spires of thrilling, varied blues. So now there was the old 'island bed' border, filled with July and August flowers, unstaked and free; and the new, more conventional May/June border, backed by old roses on a fence. The next move was to scrap the fence, and to transplant the roses.

The truth is, it is nicer to walk along a gravel path without a fence restricting the view on one side, and without exuberant roses forcing you to bend double, or decide to go another way. A gravel path to a cottage door should be softened on either side with pretty edging plants, like the purple-leaved bugle, *Ajuga reptans*, and alpine strawberries and heuchera and spiderwort and lamb's ears and bachelors' buttons. Ideally, it should have one or two arches over it, wreathed in climbers, rather than shrub roses trained on wires. Moreover, though the roses put up with competition from the apple trees, the apple trees began to signal that they might do better without the roses. We had made that old mistake that is so easy to spot in other people's gardens: we had over-planted. Our imaginations had failed to encompass the size to which our plants might one day grow. So now we are in the process of moving our old roses. 'Céleste' and 'Charles de Mills' and 'Kathleen Harrop' and 'Stanwell Perpetual' have already moved. The astonishing thing is that they have not only survived, they have prospered. However much you slaughter the roots and slash the top growth in the back-breaking business of levering these huge old specimens out of the earth, it seems you are unlikely to kill them, though they may look mutilated for a year and will appreciate frequent watering. It turns out that to move a rose to nice new quarters is the best way to prolong its life. It makes new roots, new top growth, it is rejuvenated.

A wide circle of shrub roses has formed below the pond as an extension of the formal rose garden above it. The old friends have taken their places there, joined by new albas, damasks and centifolias. There is the damask 'Ispahan', which has one of the longest flowering seasons amongst old roses; it sometimes offers a bright pink flower or two in August, and even when not in bloom is a tall, graceful shrub. There is the centifolia 'Petite de Hollande', neat as its name, and of the same sugar pink as 'Ispahan'. Then there is the slender Bourbon 'Mme Pierre Oger', the exquisitely shaped rose with concentric circles of concave petals like shells, sometimes unexpectedly dotted with deep pink but prettiest in its characteristic paler phase. There are three more albas, with matt grey leaves, to join 'Céleste': the warmer pink 'Königin von Dänemark', the paler 'Maiden's Blush', clustered and convoluted, and the almost single old white rose, *Alba semi-plena*. The vigorous hybrid musk 'Penelope' with creamy-peach flowers, grows out of the grass lower down the slope; so does le Grice's charming perpetual-flowering shrub rose with glossy leaves: 'Pearl Drift', pearl white as its name implies though its parents were the yellow 'Mermaid' and the pink 'New Dawn'. Finally there is the cool pink hybrid rugosa 'Sarah Van Fleet', with its heady rugosa scent. All these young roses wear cylinders of wire netting round their stems in winter to protect them from the baby rabbits that find them so delicious. No apple trees are near; the ground slopes gently; I look forward to a wide wreath of rose shrubs circling a sunny lawn.

Between the roses, once again, other things are planted: bearded irises in lavender blue, primrose yellow, white and velvet brown; sharp green euphorbias, apricot foxgloves and the occasional towering silver scotch thistle. Beneath the purple 'Charles de Mills', a fiercely magenta centaurea with grey leaves, a refugee from the original herbaceous border, has finally found a home. Beneath 'Céleste', a band of *Ceratostigma plumbaginoides* covers the soil and comforts us with bright blue flowers amongst leaves that turn bright red when all the other flowers are over in October. At the base of sugar pink 'Ispahan' are round bushes of rue, *Ruta graveolens* 'Jackman's Blue'.

What else can fit in? I ask myself. For this is another of the gardener's characteristics: acquisitiveness. Horticultural hopefulness shades into greed. It is no longer a case of filling gaps in this garden. Rather it is a case of contriving gaps into which to fit the latest plump and peaty rootball. I have now contrived a place for a mulberry tree – the very thing I said 'No' to in Chapter III. There the little pot-grown sapling stands, right in the middle of the lawn. I must have wafts of mock orange blossom blowing over the garden in July, so a young plant of *Philadelphus* 'Belle Etoile' is fitted in amongst the circle of old roses. I see a little plant of *Hydrangea sargentiana* with its enormous furry leaves, and decide it will keep *Hydrangea paniculata* company near the wood. But where can I find an adequate place for *Hydrangea villosa*, the beautiful spreading hydrangea with the long, pointed grey leaves and lavender flowers? It looks best against a sheltered wall and my sheltered walls are full. And why did I not fit in an espaliered pear against the tallest cottage wall, as a visitor suggested twenty years ago? All this is like a well-fed gourmet dreaming of food. Dreaming is one of the most pleasant forms of gardening. But all my gardening here has been a drive to realise a dream, and that, for me, is what the joy consists in: a vision forms in the mind's eye, and one attempts to make it real.

The vision we had, on our first visit here, of the reversed view, is now real. Not only is our whole southern hedge demolished or cut low, but this year we arranged with a neighbouring farmer to trim the overgrown hedge beyond, that runs along the far side of the meadow at the foot of our garden. The view is now wide open, stretching across half a dozen flat meadows to the river, and ending only with the gently rising, wooded ground, distant and misty on the further bank. And this casts doubt on our whole garden lay-out: the view is now so good, it seems we should have directed all our lines of vision, all our flower beds, towards it. I am busy now realigning things, making adjustments. I have extended the herbaceous border right up to the hedge round the peach garden, and cut a wide grassy swathe obliquely through it, leading the eye towards the view. (See Plate 1.) An architectural *Yucca filamentosa* stands on either side of this grassy path, helping to make the point.

We have our so-called vista, the gap in the hedge marked at each side by a Dawyck beech. And this looks good from the west-facing seat beneath the sitting-room window where we sit drinking tea on summer afternoons. From this position a beautifully rounded hedgerow oak is framed by fastigiate beeches, exactly central. But in a wide garden like this the lines of vision continually change as you walk about in it. I rise from my seat, stroll across the front lawn with my cup of tea, and the beeches no longer frame the oak; one of them has disappeared behind a hedge, and the other is left alone, marooned in the boundary, a foolish, inconsequential exclamation mark in all that flat space. Looking at a garden is not like looking at a picture; it exists in three-dimensional space, and the design must take into account the wandering viewer. The problem was too difficult for me; I consulted a friend who was training to be a landscape architect. She made sketches, looked with seeing eyes, and found a simple answer: plant another Dawyck beech, a third, beside the one which, from some viewpoints, looked alone. Twin beeches look intended where a solitary one looks accidental; a pair of beeches on one side of the vista and a single one on the other also look good – less stiffly symmetrical than the old arrangement. I had aimed at a formality that might be perfect in a château on the Loire, or carried out with a pair of cypresses against an Italian sky, but was inappropriate in this rural scene where garden aims to merge into meadows.

The simplest answer is nearly always the best; dreams for the future must not be allowed to replace simplicity with complex distractions; one must remember what one's original aims were. Our aims were to make a country garden, filled with scented, old-fashioned flowers, subdivided into different compartments, framing our thatched cottage on the one hand and belonging, on the other, to the agricultural scene. It must have privacy and serenity, sheltered places for garden seats where one might sit and look.

We have six garden seats, all acquired second-hand over the years at local auction sales; five of them are traditional slatted hardwood; and one, by the pond, is white-painted cast iron. They fit more permanently and quietly into their places than upholstered florals or striped dacron chairs might do, though they may be less comfortable. For dreamy comfort, when the gnats allow, there is a string hammock slung between an oak and an ash in the wood. In all these places I sit, or lie, and survey the scene. At these moments I have trained myself not to observe the bad but to concentrate my eyes upon the good.

The unplanned, chance effects give the greatest joy: the two clumps of yellow crown imperials seen against a background of clipped yew in spring; a spike of tawny red *Rodgersia pinnata* rising in front of the purple-leaved sumach, *Cotinus coggygria*, beyond the pond; self-sown flowers in lilac and purple grouping themselves amongst green and golden herbs: the herbs are the golden marjoram and the green-gold lemon balm, and the flowers are the rosy purple honesty, growing out of the path, the pavings, cracks in the concrete, corners of the yew hedge, everywhere it is allowed, and the little, prolific *Viola labradorica*, with plum-dark leaves and lilac flowers, spreading between stones; big cushions of grander violas in mauve, purple, white and gold gratuitously bind together the unplanned colour-scheme. One of the assets of a sandy soil is the readiness with which plants seed themselves in it. They do not always get it right; when I think I can do better, then I move them. If I think of an improvement for next year I try to make a written note of it, otherwise it will fade away with the flowers and the seasons and the changing light.

In the end, it is the ever-changing nature of a garden which holds the gardener captive; if things look unimaginative and inadequate at noon, they will have revived with the spreading shadows by tea-time. If the August grass is yellow with drought, the rains will come and in September there will be miraculous green again. If one season is bare, the next will be abundant. I am, of course, no longer content that our garden should have flowers in it during the school holidays; I aim towards that captivating possibility, the all-the-year-round garden. It is not as difficult as it sounds. If you have daffodils and flowering fruit trees, spring will look after itself; in April, our garden is carried by its fringes and ditches where the naturalised daffodils grow. In May, the apple and cherry blossom are enough, together with the smell of newly-cut grass, for in May the meadow grass grows at a prodigious rate and the very air is full of promise and of birdsong, with blackbirds and thrushes and robins in the trees. In June and July there are roses; but in August we would be dull

if we had not concentrated all our original planting on this
month alone, with the herbaceous border of late summer
flowers, so that the drabbest, dustiest season in most gardens is
our best. In September there is a lull, and a minor repeat of roses;
in October it is above all the stretches of beech and hornbeam
and maple hedges in their warming autumn leaves that redeem
the garden, and in winter we are saved again by hedges: dark
yew against warm brown beech, with the brilliant stems of the
pollarded willows in a row beyond. When it snows, the yew is
black, giving security and definition and the final triumph of
simplicity in the unifying white.

To cultivate an ambitious garden round a house you do not
live in all the time may seem wrong-headed, if not crazed. 'How
do you do it?' people ask, meaning, '*Why* do you do it?' The
answer to the first question is: 'By allowing it to look unkempt.'
The answer to the second question is: 'Because I love it.'

Many people only tend their gardens at weekends, but there is
a special joy in regularly going away from a garden and coming
back to it again: it lies in the moment of arrival when you rush
from the car to discover transformation. For every week of
spring and summer will mount a transformation scene: something new will have burst into bloom during the days of absence.
One night in spring we arrived at dusk to find the apple blossom
had come out while we were away, and there it was, scenting
the air, more substantial than cherry blossom and more tran-
sient. We caught it at its peak, luminous white with the moon
just rising. It was the old thrill of the cow parsley discovered all
round the cottage in our first Norfolk spring.

My husband is retired now, and has more time to spend here.
The strimmer hums along the edges of the borders and ditches,
the grass is not allowed to grow long, we have a heavy, two-
stroke hedge trimmer with a 31 in. blade which he uses in short
bouts while I anxiously hold the steps. It is not really a cottage
garden any more and it has two gardeners at work in it: one neat

and energetic (my husband), one obsessed and dreamy (myself).

The cottage bookshelves are full of musty children's books and the chests-of-drawers are stuffed with hand-made dolls, cobbled together in long-past summer holidays. But 'Action Man' no longer parachutes from the upstairs windows and the canvas paddling pool has long since served as a cover for the ride-on mower. The little son who helped me dig the pond now lives in Amsterdam, returning to the cottage for fleeting visits, when he wields whatever powered tools are waiting until his shoulders ache. The two little girls who found special flints in the garden or wept over dead goldfish are now busy London journalists who love the cottage and its garden but live elsewhere, returning for odd weekends when it's a case of 'singing: – "O, how beautiful!" and sitting in the shade' – or in the sun, if possible.

For the twenty-two years this story covers I have been mixing gardening with English literature and have been able to recite long chunks of poetry under my breath while weeding deep in the herbaceous border. A few weeks ago I, too, retired – from teaching, not from gardening.

We do not allow ourselves a sidelong glance at that final, distantly-looming question: 'How long will you be able to keep this up?' But if this cottage finds itself in the estate agents' hands again one day, I hope the 'Particulars' will devote a special paragraph to the garden, the trees, the hedges and the view.

Index